KARATE-DO

## "KARATE NI SENTE NASHI"
"There is no first strike in Karate" – Gichin Funakoshi

MY TRADITIONAL KARATE PATHWAY
# STRENGTH, SKILL AND KNOWLEDGE

道場

# THIS IS MY DOJO!

## My Karate School (and start Date):

## My Sensei:

## My Senpai(s):

ADD YOUR KARATE SCHOOL PHOTO, SCHOOL LOGO OR A STICKER HERE

MY TRADITIONAL KARATE PATHWAY
**STRENGTH, SKILL AND KNOWLEDGE**

# THIS IS MY DOJO!

## What do I want to Achieve in Karate:

## My Otagai(s):

MY TRADITIONAL KARATE PATHWAY
# STRENGTH, SKILL AND KNOWLEDGE

## DOJO KUN - 道場訓

### HITOTSU: JINKAKU KANSEI NI TSUTOMURU KOTO
**DEVELOP GOOD CHARACTER**
*Strive for the development of your character*
一、人格完成に努むること

### HITOTSU: MAKOTO NO MICHI O MAMORU KOTO
**BE TRUTHFUL & SINCERE**
*Strive to develop the virtues of Truth and Sincerity*
一、誠の道を守ること

### HITOTSU: DORYOKU NO SEICHIN O YASHINAU KOTO
**APPLY MAXIMUM EFFORT**
*Cultivate the spirit of perseverance*
一、努力の精神を養うこと

### HITOTSU: REIGI O OMONZURU KOTO
**BE RESPECTFUL TO OTHERS**
*Honour the principles of good etiquette*
一、礼儀を重んずること

### HITOTSU: KEKKI NO YU O IMASHIMURU KOTO
**MAINTAIN SELF-CONTROL**
*Guard against Reckless and Violent behaviour*
一、血気の勇を戒むること

MY TRADITIONAL KARATE PATHWAY
# STRENGTH, SKILL AND KNOWLEDGE

# INDEX

- THIS IS MY DOJO!
- DOJO KUN – CODE OF CONDUCT
- LET'S START LEARNING KARATE
- BRIEF HISTORY OF KARATE
- WELCOME TO THE DOJO
- TOOLS AND TARGETS
- BELTS AND RANKINGS
- DACHI WAZA - STANCES
- ASHI WAZA - FOOT WORK
- KOSHI WAZA – HIP TECHNIQUE
- UKE WAZA – BLOCKS
- ZUKI WAZA – PUNCHES
- UCHI WAZA – STRIKES
- GERI-WAZA – KICKS
- KUMITE - SPARRING
- KATA
- KARATE VOCABULARY
- MY GOALS
- 20 GUIDING PRINCIPALS OF KARATE-DO
- MY KARATE JOURNAL

MY TRADITIONAL KARATE PATHWAY
# STRENGTH, SKILL AND KNOWLEDGE

## LET'S START LEARNING
# KARATE

**Welcome!**

What a great choice to start learning Karate. You have taken your first steps in your Karate journey that we'll hope lasts a lifetime. Learning and practising Karate can benefit and assist you in so many levels and with so many other aspects of your life besides the obvious Martial-Art and self-defence skills. Karate's main focus has always been on personal development and improvement of character as a way of life. Hence the Karate-'Do', The 'Way' of Karate. Training Karate will improve your self-confidence, stress handling and conflict resolution skills, it will strengthen your body and mind to better deal with various challenges in life. We truly welcome you to one of the largest Martial-Art and Sport families in a world with over 100 million practitioners. Oss!

As a beginner, this booklet is made just for you!
We hope it will make the start of your Karate journey a little bit easier and make you feel more at home at the Dojo from the start. In next few chapters we will introduce you to some of our most common basic techniques, related vocabulary, and Dojo etiquette. All, and much more you need to know to start your journey. The purpose of this book is to familiarise you with the techniques and support your learning at the Dojo under the supervision of qualified Martial Art teachers with appropriate expertise and experience. Remember, safety first, yours and others. Don't attempt any of the techniques without supervision and advice from a qualified teacher as they might result in damage, cause injury, or hurt.

MY TRADITIONAL KARATE PATHWAY
STRENGTH, SKILL AND KNOWLEDGE

# BRIEF HISTORY OF KARATE

Modern Karate as we know it today has develop and evolved for centuries. It originated from the southern tip of modern Japan called Okinawa (Old Ryukyu Kingdom) as an indigenous Ryukyuan martial art called 'Te' (Hand). 'Te' was mixed and heavily shaped by the Chinese martial arts from as early as 1300's when the Chinese merchants and envoys first started visiting the islands. Hence, it became locally known as 'Kara-Te', meaning 'Chinese Hand'. It's best-known 'styles' were called Shuri-te, Naha-te, and Tomari-te, respectively named after the cities they emerged from.

Bans on practising martial arts and rulings concerning bladed weaponry by the King of Ryukyu Kingdom in late 1400's and the continued ban on arms after the Japanese samurai invasion in 1609, are said to have played important part and contributed to the evolution of Karate as unarmed martial art. During these periods Karate was a 'hidden martial art' and only practised in secret by the locals.

In early 1900's Karate was introduced in Okinawan school system as an official form of physical exercise and a bit later, it was formally introduced in a mainland Japan as 'KARATE-DO', The Way of 'Empty-Hand', instead of 'Chinese-Hand' to appease the political and cultural climate. There it adopted the use of white uniforms and the colour belt grading system that were both used by the Judokas. It was officially recognised as a 'Martial Art' by the Japanese government in 1926.

In early and mid 1900's the methods of teaching Karate in Japan were systemised, modernised and formalised, and the first 'official' forms of Karate competition were established. The first All Japan Karate championships was held in Tokyo 1957.

MY TRADITIONAL KARATE PATHWAY
STRENGTH, SKILL AND KNOWLEDGE

# BRIEF HISTORY OF KARATE

...Continued

Karate, as we know it today, as Martial Art and in its 'Sport' form, has widely spread all around the world and is, in its all forms, the biggest Martial Art family and one of the biggest Sport families in a World with an estimated 100 million practitioners.

In the 'World Karate Family', the four most active and popular siblings are the Shotokan, Wado-ryu, Shito-ryu, and Goju-ryu. That are all, amongst many others, rooted, connected, and originate from the same ancient Okinawan 'Te'. They all cultivate the flame and carry the torch of Te' and Kara-Te' forward. They all share the connection to the past and keep the Karate-Do, 'The Way of Karate' with its teachings, history, traditions, and philosophy alive.

When you step through that door into your Dojo, or are invited to enter any other Dojo, respect their ways and traditions and keep your mind open. Explore, discover, keep learning, and enjoy your journey.

Oss!

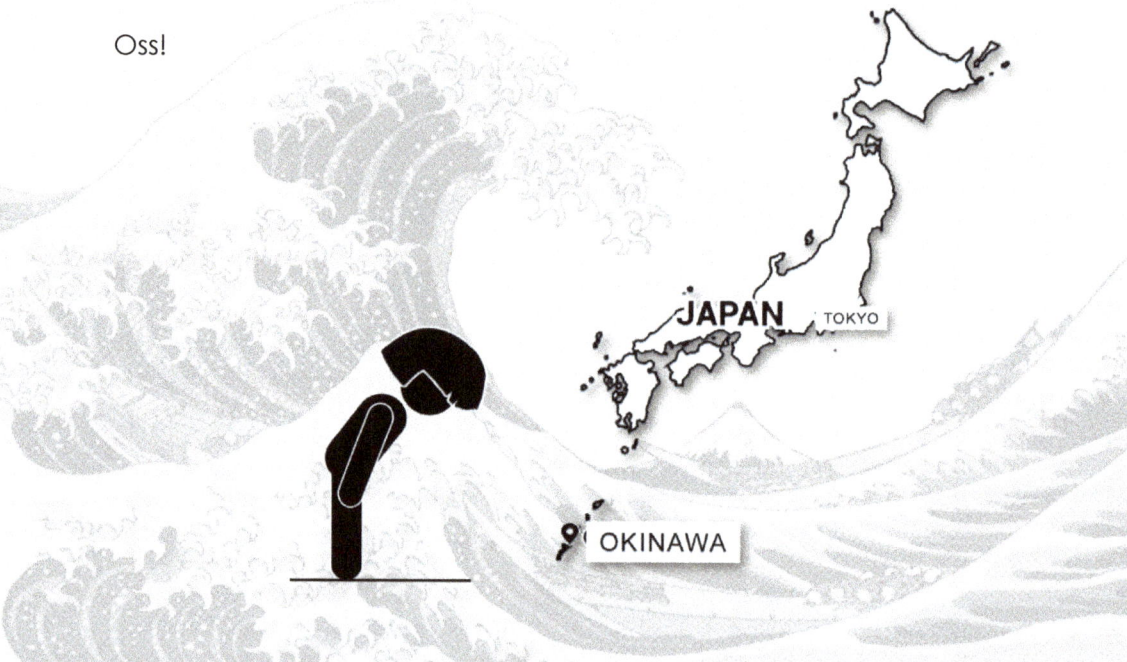

MY TRADITIONAL KARATE PATHWAY
# STRENGTH, SKILL AND KNOWLEDGE

# WELCOME TO THE DOJO!

## Enter the Dojo

When joining or entering a Dojo, you should expect to find a safe and family friendly professional learning place with accredited and certified teachers with an appropriate expertise and experience, where all the students and teachers are at all times treated with respect and courtesy. We recommend finding a Karate Dojo that teaches Traditional Japanese Karate, adheres to its code of conduct and values (Dojo Kun), promotes friendship, diversity, and the spirit of learning. It is also expected that students in their character and actions, in and outside of the Dojo, will positively reflect those values, their Club and Karate-Do.

*"karate-dō wa rei ni hajimari rei ni owaru koto o wasuruna"*
Karate begins and ends with courtesy and respect
(Gichin Funakoshi).

MY TRADITIONAL KARATE PATHWAY

# STRENGTH, SKILL AND KNOWLEDGE

# WELCOME TO THE DOJO!

## At the Dojo

**You will Meet:**

- Sensei: The main teacher
- Senpai: Other teachers and higher-grade students
- Otagai: Fellow students
- Kohai: Lower grade student

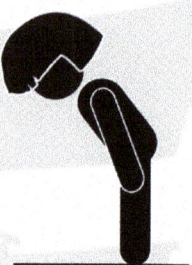

**You are expected to:**

- Be Punctual.
- If you arrive late, wait for permission from Sensei to join the class.
- When arriving at the training area, bow to the front to show respect.
- When arriving, greet your teacher/s (bow).
- Be respectful and courteous at all times.
- Pay attention and not to distract other students from learning.
- When pairing up, greet your training partners at the start and at the end with a bow to show respect and that we value their help in our learning.
- When teacher has given you some advice, instructed or helped you, it is courteous to bow and say 'Oss!'. 'Oss' is a specific respectful Karate expression to show that you've heard the instructions, appreciate their time, help, and advice, and to say Thank you!
- Wear a Dogi (Uniform) with an Obi (Belt).
- if you need to fix your belt or Dogi you don't do it facing Sensei or the front of the Dojo, always turn around.
- Leave your shoes outside the training area.
- Have clean and neat personal appearance.
- If applicable, have your long hair pulled back.
- Have clean and trimmed finger-and toenails (safety matter).
- Not to wear any type of jewellery, bands, or watches.
- Not to bring in or eat any food at the Dojo. (Water bottles are ok)
- After the class it is good manners to ensure the Dojo is left clean after us.

**MY TRADITIONAL KARATE PATHWAY**
# STRENGTH, SKILL AND KNOWLEDGE

# WELCOME TO THE DOJO!

## In The Class

**At the start, you will:**
Line up (Seiretsu) according to the belt rankings.
Stand in an attention stance (Musubi Dachi)
Pay attention to the Teacher (Sensei)
Follow the class Captains lead and call, to:
   **Seiza** (Kneel down in a sitting position).
   **Mokuso** (a moment of silence and calm breathing to clear your mind).
   **Rei** (Show respect to the teachers and other students by traditional bowing). "Shomen Ni Rei, Sensei Ni Rei (Oss), Senpai Katani Rei (Oss) and Otagai Ni Rei (Oss)".

**When the class is in progress, you will:**
Learn from, and train with the three foundations of Karate Teaching:

**KIHON**: Basic techniques.  Stances, footwork, blocks, punches, and kicks.
**KATA**:   Patterns that connect techniques, stances, and movements.
**KUMITE**: Practise sparring/ exercise the techniques with a partner.

**At the end, you will:**
Line up again, exactly in a same order than in a start
Stand in the attention stance
Pay attention to the teacher
Follow the class Captains lead and call to:
   **Seiza** (Kneel).
   **Mokuso** (a moment of silence and calm breathing to clear your mind) .
   **Dojo Kun** Listen and repeat after the Captain recite 'Code of Conduct'.
   **Rei** (Show respect by traditional bowing).

Stand up and thank the teachers for the class by bowing (Sensei and Senpai). This is to show respect and that we've valued their help in our learning.

MY TRADITIONAL KARATE PATHWAY
STRENGTH, SKILL AND KNOWLEDGE

# TOOLS AND TARGETS

## KARA (Empty) - TE (Hand) – DO (Way)

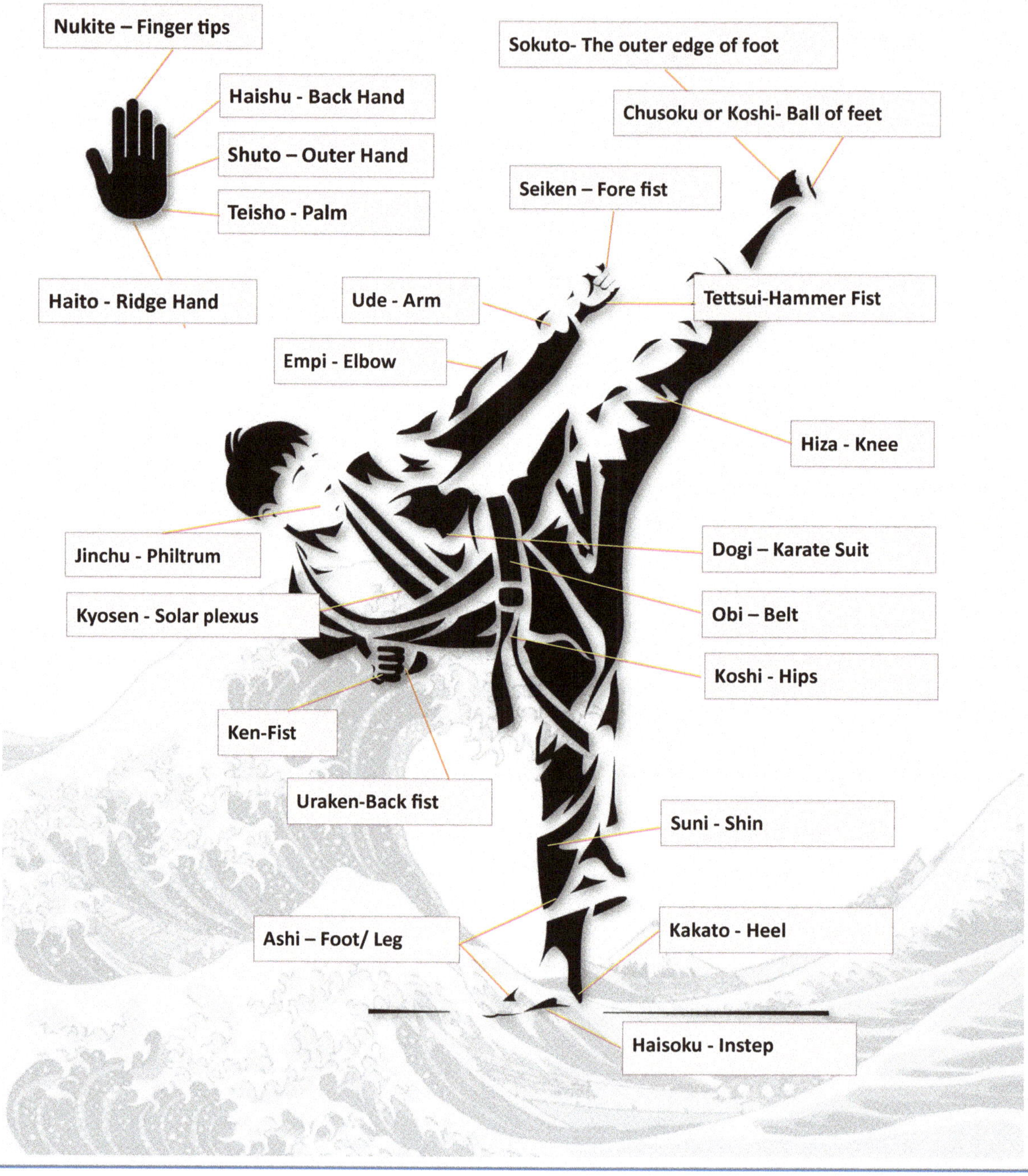

- Nukite – Finger tips
- Haishu - Back Hand
- Shuto – Outer Hand
- Teisho - Palm
- Haito - Ridge Hand
- Ude - Arm
- Empi - Elbow
- Jinchu - Philtrum
- Kyosen - Solar plexus
- Ken - Fist
- Uraken - Back fist
- Ashi – Foot/ Leg
- Sokuto - The outer edge of foot
- Chusoku or Koshi - Ball of feet
- Seiken – Fore fist
- Tettsui - Hammer Fist
- Hiza - Knee
- Dogi – Karate Suit
- Obi – Belt
- Koshi - Hips
- Suni - Shin
- Kakato - Heel
- Haisoku - Instep

MY TRADITIONAL KARATE PATHWAY
# STRENGTH, SKILL AND KNOWLEDGE

# BELTS AND RANKINGS

## Kyu & Dan

The 'colour' belt ranks are called 'Kyu' and progress from 10th Kyu (White belt), up to the 1st Kyu (Brown belt). The Black belt levels are called Dan, and they progress from 1st Dan upwards to 10th. Generally, the order of belt colours is as pictured below. However, different styles and clubs do have variations in colours to suite their specific ranking systems. Ranks are earned/ achieved through skill assessment and grading tests that are based on a set skill, knowledge, and attendance criterion for each level.

**Colour Belts - Kyu**

3rd to 1st Kyu
Brown

4th Kyu
Purple or Red

5th Kyu
Blue

6th Kyu
Green

7th Kyu
Orange

8th Kyu
Yellow

10-9th Kyu
White

**Competition colours – AKA/ AO**

Red represent the 'AKA' and Blue the other competitor, 'AO'.

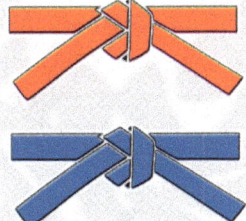

**BLACK Belts**
1st to 10th Dan

MY TRADITIONAL KARATE PATHWAY

# STRENGTH, SKILL AND KNOWLEDGE

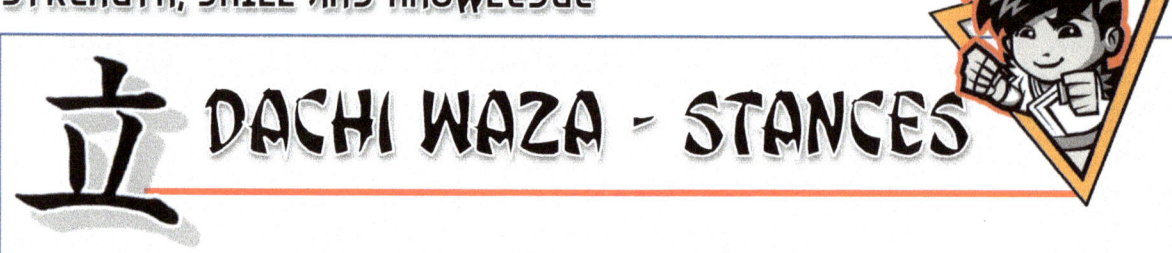

# DACHI WAZA - STANCES

Correct stances 'Dachi' are the foundation and base for all Karate techniques. With the stances, we root our feet to the ground for strength, balance, and stability. We generate striking power, acceleration, and speed from ground up through our stances. To be able to successfully perform and deliver other techniques, you will need to learn and master the stances together with the correct footwork. The good news is, it's all based in physics and sport science, so no magic tricks or invisible forces are required, just following instructions, hard work, repetition, repetition, repetition and persistence.

With the correct stances and footwork, we can successfully control things that are crucial for effective Karate. How we achieve our acceleration, speed and power. How we manage, maintain, and control our balance, distance, timing, and accuracy. How we successfully deliver a technique, or shift a threatening situation into our advantage, all depend on our abilities to use and manipulate those stances and footwork with the other techniques.

MY TRADITIONAL KARATE PATHWAY
STRENGTH, SKILL AND KNOWLEDGE

# DACHI WAZA - STANCES

## Etiquette and formal manners

## REI

A FORMAL BOW

We greet, thank, and show respect to our teachers and fellow students by bowing. We bow to the front when we enter the Dojo, and during the 'Dojo Kun' to show respect to the Dojo, to our code of conduct, to our traditions, history and the past 'pioneers' of Karate-Do. (Shomen Ni Rei). We also respond to anyone bowing to us with a bow.

**Stand and bow (From Musubi Dachi)**
Stand upright in 'Musubi Dachi' hands down to your sides, hips and shoulders squared to front. Then, in a calm manner, bow forward with a straight back and keep your eyes down. (As we trust and respect the person, we keep our eyes down). Traditionally, lower your rank or age is, deeper the bow goes.

**Sit and bow (From Seiza).**
From your kneeling position. Place the palm of your left hand to the floor in a front of your left knee, then repeat the same with your right hand. Bow forward with a straight back without lifting your behind off the legs, lower your forehead down and close to but, not touching the floor. Come back up in a reverse order.

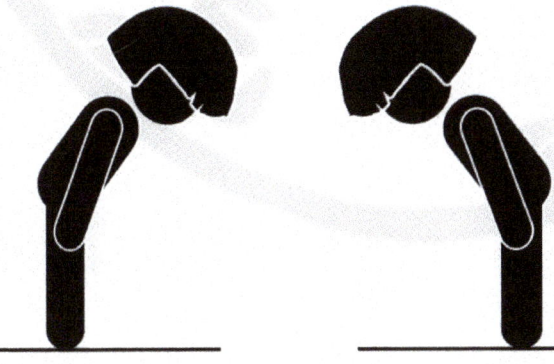

MY TRADITIONAL KARATE PATHWAY
STRENGTH, SKILL AND KNOWLEDGE

# 立 DACHI WAZA - STANCES

## Etiquette and formal manners

### SEIZA

KNEEL – 'PROPER SITTING OR TO SIT 'CORRECTLY''

A respectful traditional Japanese sitting position where we meditate (*Mokuso), pay attention, listen, recite Dojo-Kun and bow to Shomen, Sensei, Sempai and Otagai according to the traditions.

Start by standing in Musubi Dachi. Take a small step back with your left leg and kneel down by first placing your left knee on a floor and then your right knee right next to it. (Men's knees can be two fist widths apart). Sit down on a top of your feet and place your left big toe on a top of your right big toe. Rest your hands on your thighs, (open hands, palms down). Keep an upright posture with relaxed shoulders and breath calmly.

*Mokuso', is a moment of calm breathing and silence with closed eyes that is used to clear our minds (ready for the class). After the class we can use that short moment to calm down and think about today's key points.

MY TRADITIONAL KARATE PATHWAY
# STRENGTH, SKILL AND KNOWLEDGE

# 立 DACHI WAZA - STANCES

### SHIZENTAI 'NATURAL STANCES'

## MUSUBI DACHI
**FORMAL ATTENTION STANCE**

Used for formal bowing (Rei) and when lining up and paying attention to the teacher at the start and at the end of the class.

Keep hands down to your sides, with palms resting on your thighs. Stand in upright posture, hips and shoulders squared to front, keep heels together and feet open at 45° angle. Weight 50/50 on both legs.

MUSUBI DACHI

HEISOKU DACHI

## HEISOKU DACHI
**FEET TOGETHER STANCE**

Informal attention stance. An upright stance used in several katas and with many techniques.

Stand in upright posture, hips and shoulders squared to front. Feet together. Weight 50/50 on both legs.

MY TRADITIONAL KARATE PATHWAY
# STRENGTH, SKILL AND KNOWLEDGE

# 立 DACHI WAZA - STANCES

## SHIZENTAI 'NATURAL STANCES'

### HEIKO DACHI
**PARALLEL STANCE, FEET STRAIGHT**

Used as a 'Ready' stance (Yoi) in Kihon, Kata and Kumite. Often used after bowing and when listening instructions or when waiting for a 'Go'/ 'Start' (Hajime) command.

A shoulder width upright stance with hips and shoulders squared to front and toes pointing straight forward. Weight 50/50 on both legs.

HEIKO DACHI

### HACHIJI DACHI
**PARALLEL STANCE FEET OPEN**

A shoulder width stance with hips and shoulders squared to front. Feet open at 45° angle. Also used as a 'Ready' stance (Yoi) in Kihon, Kata and Kumite or for paying attention. Weight 50/50 on both legs.

HACHIJI DACHI

MY TRADITIONAL KARATE PATHWAY
STRENGTH, SKILL AND KNOWLEDGE

# DACHI WAZA - STANCES

## ZENKUTSU DACHI
FRONT STANCE (ZEN-FRONT, KUTSU -BENT)

Our most common stance. Both feet are pointing forward with the back-foot angled slightly outwards at 15°. Stance should be your shoulder width wide and twice as long. Keep both heels firmly anchored to the ground and your back leg fully extended. You should feel the back leg (from heel up), pushing your hips forward. Keep your front knee aligned and bent directly over the front foot. 60% of your weight should be on a front leg. Keep an upright posture with your shoulders and hips parallel to the floor. Hips and shoulders can be squared to the front (Shomen), open at 45° (Hanmi), or rotated to a reversed position (Gyaku-Hanmi).

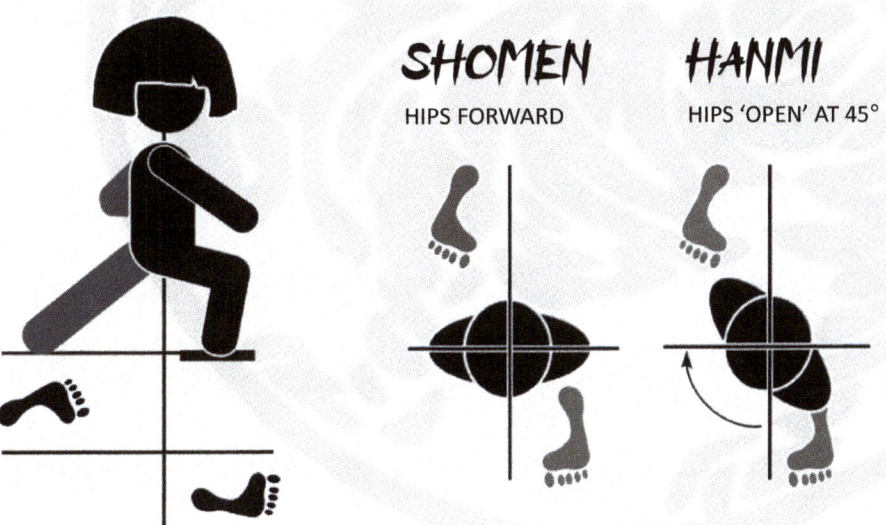

ZENKUTSU DACHI

MY TRADITIONAL KARATE PATHWAY
STRENGTH, SKILL AND KNOWLEDGE

# DACHI WAZA - STANCES

## KOKUTSU DACHI

BACK STANCE (KO-BACK, KUTSU-BENT)

This stance is mainly used for defensive techniques or combinations. Stand with both of your heels on a same line, two shoulder widths apart. Your front foot and the front knee are aligned and pointing straight forward. The back-foot and its knee are aligned and pointing directly to the side at 90° angle, or just slightly backwards. Keep both heels firmly anchored to the ground, sit on your bent back leg and push both knees slightly outwards.

Your hips and shoulders are open to the side at 45° angle (Hanmi). 70% of your weight is sitting firmly on your bent back leg. The back knee should be aligned with, and directly over the back foot. Keep your front leg slightly bent and do not 'lock' the front knee. Keep an upright posture with your shoulders and hips parallel to the floor.

KOKUTSU DACHI

### HANMI
HIPS 'OPEN' AT 45°

MY TRADITIONAL KARATE PATHWAY
STRENGTH, SKILL AND KNOWLEDGE

# 立 DACHI WAZA - STANCES

## KIBA DACHI
**HORSE RIDING STANCE**

This stance is mainly for sideways movement and techniques aimed to the side. Hips are squared to front, feet parallel two shoulder widths apart with toes pointing forward. Keep both heels firmly anchored to the ground and keep pushing your knees outwards. Sit/ squat down with your weight directly above your heels, 50/50 on both legs. Knee angle should be the same than in a front stance. Keep an upright posture with straight back. Shoulders and hips parallel to the floor.

KIBA DACHI

## SHIKO DACHI

Similar to Kiba Dachi, but your feet are open to 45° angle with toes pointing outwards. (Knees aligned with the feet).

SHIKO DACHI

MY TRADITIONAL KARATE PATHWAY
# STRENGTH, SKILL AND KNOWLEDGE

# DACHI WAZA - STANCES

## KOSA DACHI
CROSS STANCE

Often used as transitional move between stances and changes in direction. Generally, in defence, the hips are open in 'Hanmi' and in offence the hips are squared to the front 'Shomen'. Front foot is rooted flat to the ground, toes pointing forward. The front knee is aligned and bent directly over the front foot. The back foot is 'stepped' in and brought around to the outside of the front foot with its toes pointing towards the outsole of the front foot. Only the ball of the back foot is on the ground. The shin and the knee of the back foot are firmly pressed against the back of the front leg for strength and stability. Weight sitting 80% on a front foot. Keep an upright posture with shoulders and hips parallel to the floor.

KOSA DACHI

MY TRADITIONAL KARATE PATHWAY
STRENGTH, SKILL AND KNOWLEDGE

# DACHI WAZA - STANCES

## NEKO ASHI DACHI

CAT STANCE

In this stance, first square your shoulders and hips to the front and open your back foot outwards to 30-degree angle. Then sit your weight straight down on your bent back leg. Sit with a straight back, over and just slightly behind the ankle of your back foot. Next, slide the other foot forward (one foot length apart) and rest it there, heel up on the ball of the foot.

Both legs are bent, the back leg is bent at 45-degree angle with 80-90% of your weight sitting on it. Your back knee should be aligned with your back foot. Your front foot and front knee are aligned and pointing forward, the front foot is resting gently on its toes or on the ball of the foot.

NEKO ASHI DACHI

MY TRADITIONAL KARATE PATHWAY
STRENGTH, SKILL AND KNOWLEDGE

# 立 DACHI WAZA - STANCES

### RENOJI DACHI
L-SHAPE STANCE

Another upright, more 'natural' stance. Often used as transitional stance between' kata techniques and directions. Hips are open to Hanmi. Stand with both heels on a same line, one foot apart. Toes of your front foot should point straight forward and back foot to your side in a 90° angle. Keep both heels firmly anchored to the ground. Weight 60% on your back leg. Keep an upright posture, shoulders and hips parallel to the floor. (This stance, if you pull your back foot slightly in to form a 'T-shape with your feet, is called '**TEIJI DACHI**').

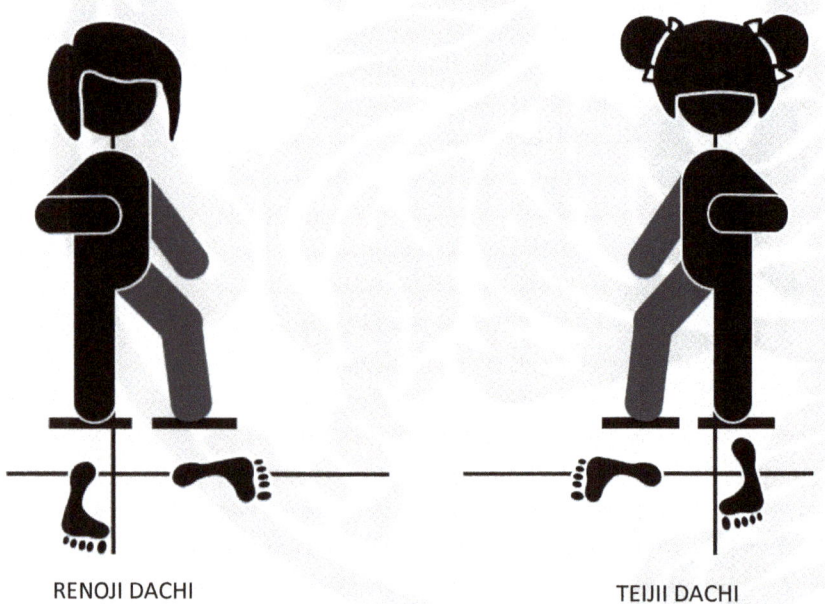

RENOJI DACHI                TEIJII DACHI

Worth to research: Kamae Dachi, Hizakutsu Dachi, Ashi Dachi, Tsuru-Ashi-Dachi, Sagi-Ashi-Dachi, Fudo-Dachi, Sanchin Dachi and postures like Ryoken Koshi Kamae (Two fists on a hip posture).

MY TRADITIONAL KARATE PATHWAY
# STRENGTH, SKILL AND KNOWLEDGE

# DACHI WAZA

## MY NOTES & KEY POINTS

Attach your notes, pictures, scribble or write something important you've learned here.

MY TRADITIONAL KARATE PATHWAY
STRENGTH, SKILL AND KNOWLEDGE

# 腰 KOSHI WAZA - HIPS

Hip movement, hip rotation, and correct alignment are essential to all our techniques, stances and footwork. Learn to control and drive your moves with the hips and feel the connection from 'heel up' to your hips. Practise using your hips and abdomen with your steps and turns by pushing and turning your body 'from' the hips and driving them from your 'core'. With practise, you will learn to support and strengthen your, moves, blocks, kicks and punches with your hips and core.

Don't underestimate the importance of using and 'conditioning' your hips.

Generally in offence the hips are squared to the front in Shomen, and in defence they are generally open to your side at 45 degree angle in Hanmi. The position where our hips are rotated to the opposite side is called 'Gyaku-Hanmi', a 'reversed hip' position (Try this with reverse side Uchi-Uke).

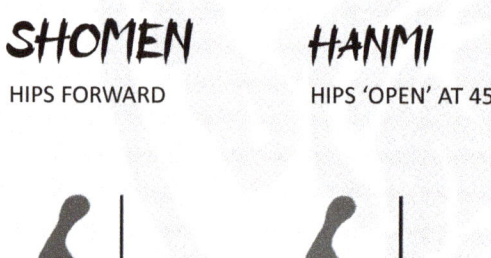

## SHOMEN
HIPS FORWARD

## HANMI
HIPS 'OPEN' AT 45°

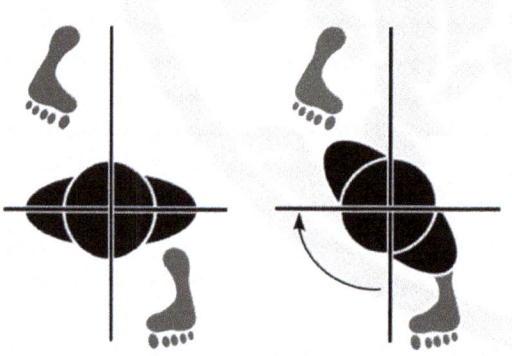

Practise the hip rotation and condition your hips by standing in a Zenkutsu Dachi and alternating the hips from Shomen to Hanmi. You can do this together with any block and punch combination. Assist the move and rotation with a proper Hikite (Retuning hand). Keep upright, don't lean, and keep your hips and shoulders parallel to the floor. Keep your front knee stationary, bent over, and aligned with your foot. Keep both feet firmly rooted to the floor.

MY TRADITIONAL KARATE PATHWAY
# STRENGTH, SKILL AND KNOWLEDGE

# 足 ASHI SABAKI - FOOTWORK

Ashi means foot, and Sabaki means movement.

## Moving in a Front Stance.

Start by pushing your front knee and hips forward. Bring your back foot in, square your hips, and transfer your entire weight to your front foot. Keep its heel anchored to the ground.

Keep sliding the back foot straight forward and past the front foot. Maintain your height and upright posture with hips and shoulders parallel to the floor and remember, 'momentum here is straight forward not up or down'. Then use your leg with the weight on it to push your hips and core strongly forward (push from heel up) and extend to full Zenkutsu Dachi.

When moving backwards, bring your front foot back in, square your hips and transfer your weight on the back leg. Keep the momentum going, push backwards and extend to full Zenkutsu Dachi

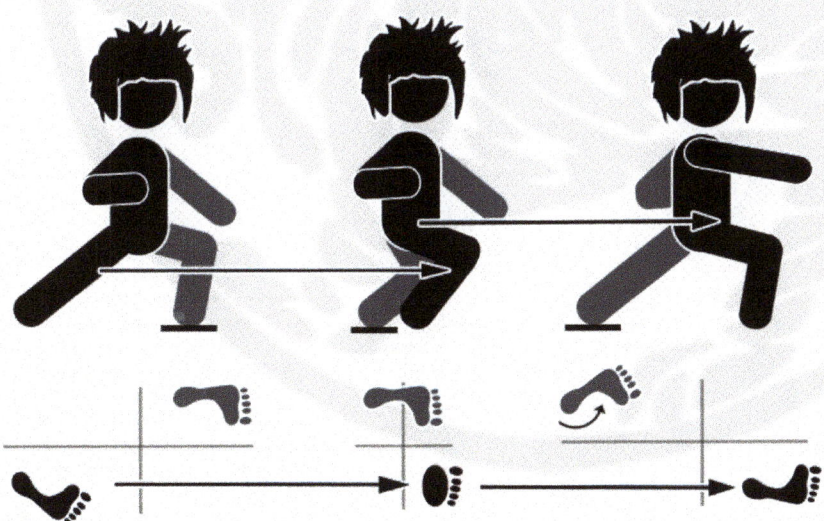

**FORWARD STEP WITH THROUGH PUNCH**

MY TRADITIONAL KARATE PATHWAY
STRENGTH, SKILL AND KNOWLEDGE

# ASHI SABAKI - FOOTWORK

## Moving in a Back Stance.

To start, push your front knee and hips forward, bring your back foot in, square your hips, and transfer your entire weight to your front foot. Keep its heel anchored to the ground.

Keep sliding the back foot straight forward and past the front foot. Maintain your height, keep an upright posture, hips and shoulders parallel to the floor and remember, 'momentum here is straight forward not up or down'. Without stopping, use the gained momentum and speed with your rotating hips (opening to Hanmi), to extend in full Kokutsu Dachi. (Rotate your hips open 'on and around' the back heel).

When moving backwards, maintain your height, keep the knees bent and an upright posture. Bring your front foot back in, square your hips and keep the weight on a same leg. Keep the momentum going, push backwards, open your hips, transfer your weight and extend to full Kokutsu Dachi

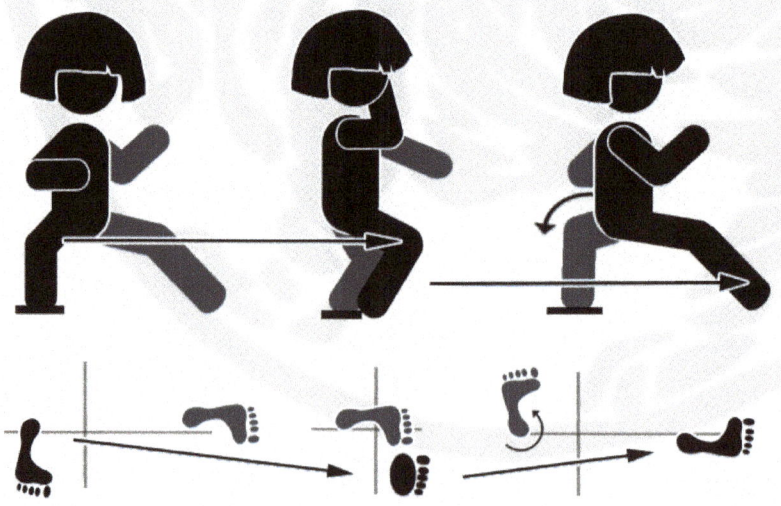

FORWARD STEP WITH KNIFE HAND BLOCK

MY TRADITIONAL KARATE PATHWAY
STRENGTH, SKILL AND KNOWLEDGE

# 足 ASHI SABAKI - FOOTWORK

## Moving in a Horse-Riding Stance.

Moving sideways. Maintain your upright upper body posture and your head height. Keep your squared shoulders and hips parallel to the floor. To start, without rotating your hips or shoulders, bring in, slide, or step your foot across, past, and right next to the other foot. Transfer your entire weight on it and keep its heel anchored to the ground. Then slide or step the other foot out to your side, extend, and transfer your weight to full Kiba Dachi.

### SURIKOMI ASHI

Like Tsugi Ashi, but you will step or slide your foot across the other one.

SIDEWAYS STEP

MY TRADITIONAL KARATE PATHWAY
STRENGTH, SKILL AND KNOWLEDGE

# 足 ASHI SABAKI - FOOTWORK

## Suri Ashi - Sliding steps:

### YORI ASHI

Expand and Contract. Move in any direction by first pushing/ sliding your leading foot out (Expanding to a longer stance), then dragging the other foot in but, not past the leading foot (Contracting back to normal size stance).

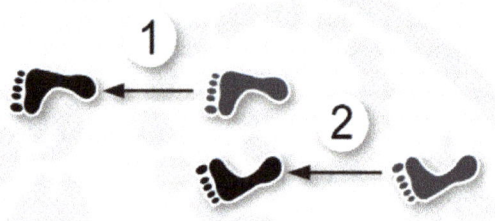

### TSUGI ASHI

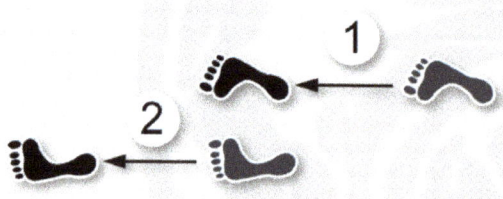

"Contract and Expand. Move in any direction by first pulling/ sliding your foot in (To a smaller stance) but, not past the other foot. Then pushing/ sliding the other foot out 'expanding' back to 'normal' stance.

### AYUMI ASHI.

Step your foot past the other. Sequence as in normal walking. In any Direction

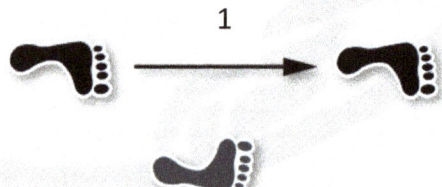

MY TRADITIONAL KARATE PATHWAY
STRENGTH, SKILL AND KNOWLEDGE

# 足 ASHI SABAKI - FOOTWORK

## TURNING

### MAWATTE, (Inside Turn, on front heel)

180 Degree Turn. TURN AROUND - SHORT INSIDE TURN (CHANGES LEADING FOOT)

In this turn we lead with the back foot. During the turn, maintain your 'upright' upper body posture and your head height with shoulders and hips parallel to the floor. Keep your elbows in and your centre of gravity low.

From Zenkutsu Dachi, start moving your back foot across your back (1) and use your hips to pivot 180° around the heel of your front foot (2). Then, without stopping, push your hips forward to extend in full Zenkutsu Dachi.

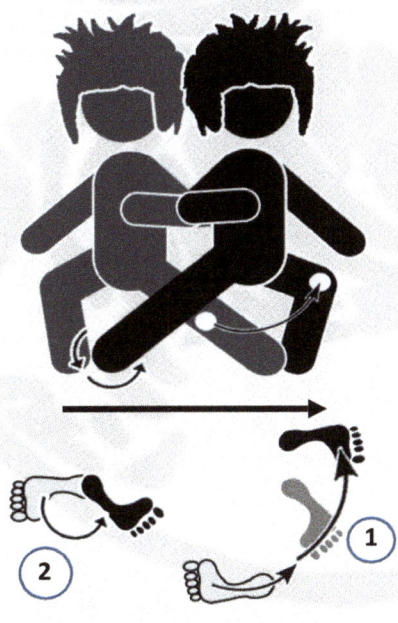

INSIDE TURN – TURN AROUND

# ASHI SABAKI - FOOTWORK

## TURNING Continued...

### D-TURN, (Outside turn, on back heel)
TURN AROUND – LONG OUTSIDE TURN (KEEPS THE SAME LEADING FOOT)

Practise from Zenkutsu Dachi: Maintain your 'upright' upper body posture and your head height with shoulders and hips parallel to the floor. Keep your centre of gravity low. Maintain your front knee angle.

In this turn, we lead with the front foot. In one continuous motion, start sliding your front foot (in a straight line) backwards and transfer (sit) your entire weight on your back foot. Without stopping, use the gained speed, momentum, and your hips to pivot around the back heel as close as you can to 180°. Keep upright, weight on your back foot/ heel and your centre of gravity low. Then push forward with your hips (from heel up) to fully extend to Zenkutsu Dachi. (Keep the back heel anchored to the ground).

D – TURN, 180 DEGREES
The 'D' in D-Turn represents the shape of the path your front foot follows.

MY TRADITIONAL KARATE PATHWAY
STRENGTH, SKILL AND KNOWLEDGE

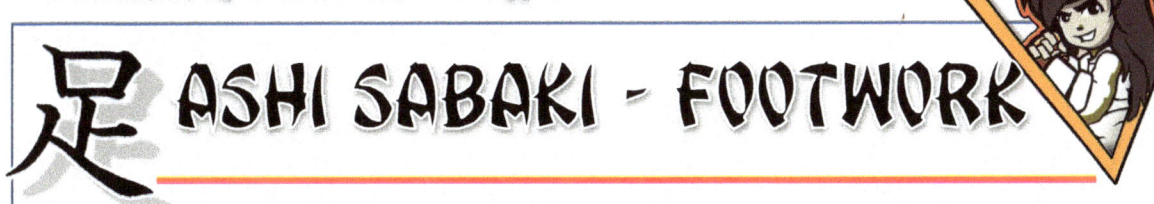

# ASHI SABAKI - FOOTWORK

## TURNING Continued...

Practice the next three turns by shifting and pivoting (Driving with your hips and turning around your heel) from full Zenkutsu Dachi with Gedan Barai through the centre of your gravity to another Zenkutsu Dachi with a Gedan Barai. Remember to keep upright, elbows in, and your weight low and centred during these turns.

### 180 Degree turn, The 'D' - turn.

Leading with a front foot and driving with the hips, pull back and pivot (From outside) around the heel of your back foot. 'D' due the shape of the path your front foot follows when turning.

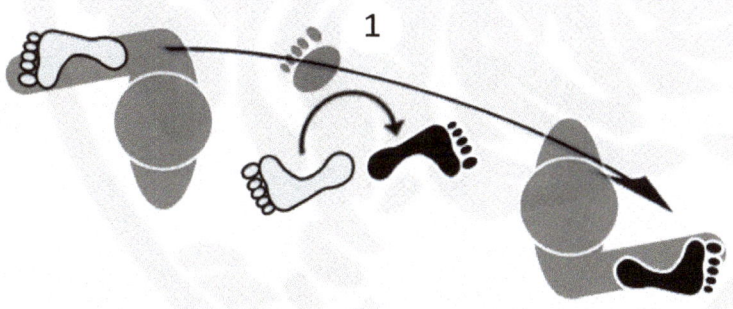

D-TURN

## ASHI SABAKI - FOOTWORK

### TURNING Continued...

### 90 Degree turn, to the side.

To the right (Migi) from a right-hand stance, or to the left (Hidari) from a left-hand stance. Leading with a front foot and driving with the hips, shift your direction directly to your side. Pivot around the heel of your back foot and extend to full stance to your side.

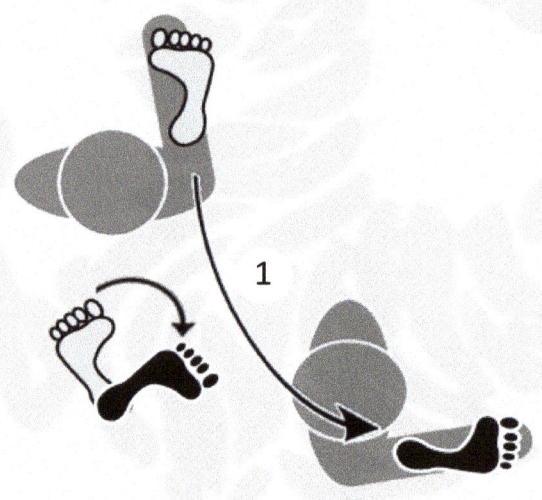

**LEFT OR RIGHT TURN**

MY TRADITIONAL KARATE PATHWAY
STRENGTH, SKILL AND KNOWLEDGE

# ASHI SABAKI - FOOTWORK

## TURNING Continued...

### 270 Degree turn, Around the back foot

In this ¾ turn, we lead with the back foot. In one continuous motion, from Zenkutsu Dachi, start moving your back foot across your back and use your hips to pivot around the heel of your front foot. Without stopping, use the gained speed, momentum, and your hips to continue pivoting as close to 270° as you can. Keep your elbows in and the centre of your gravity low. Then push forward (from heel up) and fully extend to Zenkutsu Dachi. (Keep your heel anchored to the ground). Practise this turn until you can do it in one fluid motion without losing your balance.

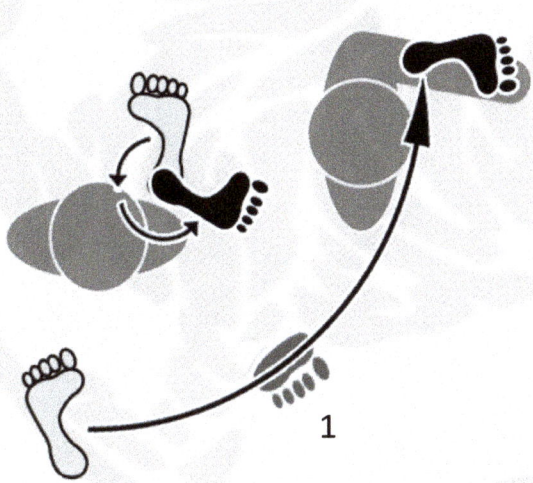

AROUND THE BACK FOOT TURN

MY TRADITIONAL KARATE PATHWAY
# STRENGTH, SKILL AND KNOWLEDGE

# ASHI SABAKI

## MY NOTES & KEY POINTS

Attach your notes, pictures, scribble or write something important you've learned here.

MY TRADITIONAL KARATE PATHWAY
STRENGTH, SKILL AND KNOWLEDGE

# ZUKI WAZA - PUNCHES

Punches, the 'Zuki' are delivered in straightforward (Thrusting) motion with the two knuckles of your index and middle finger ('Seiken)' of your tightly clenched fist (Ken). It is important to understand from the start that we control the reach of our punches with our stances and footwork, not by overextending our arms or by leaning our body. You should also keep in mind that the main contributors for your striking power are your speed and techniques, not your strength.

## 'KEN, SEIKEN, HIKITE & ZUKI

FIST, KNUCKLES, A RETURNING HAND TECHNIQUE AND PUNCH

To perform a Karate punch correctly, you will need a correctly formed fist (Ken) and learn how to perform a 'returning hand' technique (Hikite).

## KEN/ SEIKEN

FORMING A FIST

Stand in Heiko Dachi with squared hips. Fully extend both of your arms with open hands directly in a front of your chest at Chudan level (Just below the shoulder level, in a front of your solar plexus) with palms facing down (Thumbs in). Then without moving your hands, wrists, or arms, roll your fingers in to form a fist, and seal them with the thumbs on a top of the fingers. Ensure the top of the wrist and fist are levelled straight like a ruler and the 'Seiken', (The two knuckles of the index and middle finger) are pointing directly to the 'target'. Keep the fists together side by side.

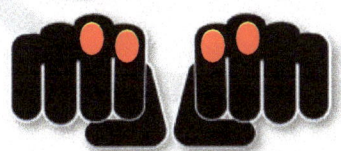

'Seiken' are the two knuckles of the index and middle finger.

MY TRADITIONAL KARATE PATHWAY
# STRENGTH, SKILL AND KNOWLEDGE

# 突き ZUKI WAZA - PUNCHES

## Continued... KEN, SEIKEN, HIKITE & ZUKI

### LEARNING HIKITE
**RETURNING HAND**

With both of your straight arms and clenched fists still directly in a front of your chest, without changing their height or alignment, start the 'Hikite' (Returning Hand Technique) by rolling your right fist out until the back of the fist is facing down. From here, pull the fist (with your elbow) straight backwards. Keep your elbow in and ensure your arm is brushing against the side of your body, pull it back until your clenched fist is on your side with the back of it still facing downwards and knuckles facing the target. Keep your elbow tucked in. In this position, when your hips are squared to the front, your fist should have a direct line to the target.

'Hikite' should be as fast and 'snappy' as the punch or the block performed with it. Imagine using your elbow to hit an opponent directly behind you.

FIST TURN

HIKITE, 'RETURNING HAND'

# 突き ZUKI WAZA – PUNCHES

## Continued... KEN, SEIKEN, HIKITE & ZUKI

### LEARNING ZUKI/TSUKI
THE PUNCH

To start, keep an upright posture, shoulders and hips squared to the front. Move your fist from your side towards the target in a straight line. (Drawn from your elbow, through the fist, to the target). Ensure the side of your arm brushes along your side and keep your elbow in. Once your elbow leaves the side of your body, in one 'snapping' motion, fully extend your arm and roll your fist back in (Knuckles up) and deliver the punch with the 'Seiken'. In this exercise, your fist should end up back in our starting position with the two fists and arms side by side, thumbs together.

When punching, keep upright, don't lean forward or overextend your arm. Keep the punch straight, elbow in and don't allow your elbow or fist to 'circle out'. Control your striking distance with your stance and footwork, not by leaning forward or overextending the arm or shoulder.

To practise, repeat doing both the Hikite and Zuki simultaneously with opposite hands. Once you're comfortable with this technique, practise it with your emphasis on correct hip rotation (Koshi Waza) and 'Hikite' to launch, speed up and power up the punch.

CHOKU ZUKI – FRONT PUNCH

MY TRADITIONAL KARATE PATHWAY
# STRENGTH, SKILL AND KNOWLEDGE

# 突き ZUKI WAZA - PUNCHES

## CHOKU ZUKI/ OI-ZUKI
FRONT PUNCH/ THROUGH STEP PUNCH.

A straightforward punch with hips and shoulders squared to the front (Shomen). Delivered with 'Seiken'.

In **'Oi-Zuki'**, the punch is delivered on the leading foot, at the same time and together with landing a 'through step'. It combines the power and speed of the punch, the forward thrusted hips and the 'through step'. (See 'moving in Zenkutsu Dachi'). Keep your upright posture and do not 'circle out' or overextend your arm, or lean forward.

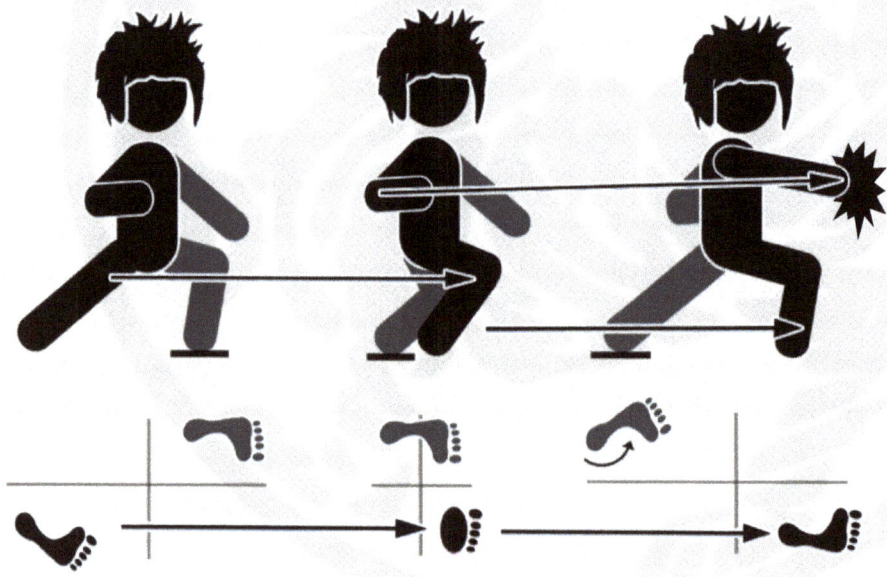

'OI ZUKI'/ LUNGE PUNCH

MY TRADITIONAL KARATE PATHWAY
# STRENGTH, SKILL AND KNOWLEDGE

# ZUKI WAZA - PUNCHES

## GYAKU ZUKI
REVERSE PUNCH

A straightforward punch with the 'Seiken' like Choku Zuki but, delivered on the 'reverse side' (back foot side). The 'Reverse' Punch is launched from and with the hips moving from 'Hanmi' to 'Shomen' and after 'landing' the front foot (if stepping through). Often as a part of fast and short combinations (Renzoku Waza) following another technique like Kizame, Jodan Oi-zuki, or a Uke-Waza, taking full advantage of the power and speed of extending back leg and the hip rotation. (Power from heel to hips).

When punching, keep upright, don't lean forward or overextend your arm. Keep the punch straight, elbow in and don't allow your elbow or fist to 'circle out'. Control your striking distance with your stance and footwork, not by leaning forward or overextending the arm or shoulder.

To practise, repeat doing both the Hikite and Zuki simultaneously with opposite hands. Once you're comfortable with this technique, practise it with your emphasis on correct hip rotation (Koshi Waza) and 'Hikite' to launch, speed up and power up the punch.

'GYAKU ZUKI' – A REVERSE PUNCH

MY TRADITIONAL KARATE PATHWAY
# STRENGTH, SKILL AND KNOWLEDGE

## 突き ZUKI WAZA - PUNCHES

### KIZAME ZUKI
'LEADING' PUNCH

Kizame-Zuki is a quick, fast, and powerful punch with 'extra reach. It's a straightforward punch delivered from the leading foot side with 'Seiken' like Choku-Zuki or Oi-Zuki but, delivered with the hips and (upright) shoulders rotated open to 'Hanmi' for extended reach. Usually delivered with extending step like in Yori-Ashi, or with a 'step through' step as in Oi-Zuki.

As with the other punches, keep upright, don't lean forward or overextend your arm. Keep the punch straight, elbow in and don't allow your elbow or fist to 'circle out'. Control your striking distance with your stance and footwork, not by leaning forward or overextending the arm or shoulder.

To practise, repeat doing the punch with the front step, Hikite and correct hip rotation.

KIZAME ZUKI

MY TRADITIONAL KARATE PATHWAY
# STRENGTH, SKILL AND KNOWLEDGE

# 打 UCHI WAZA - STRIKES

Strikes are usually delivered in a circular (arc) motion swivelled around the elbow using any parts of the hand or arms' like your palms, fingers, fists or elbows.

**TETTSUI UCHI**
HAMMER STRIKE

**NUKITE**
SPEAR HAND STRIKE

**URAKEN**
BACK FIST STRIKE

**SHUTO UCHI**
SWORD HAND STRIKE

**TEISHO**
PALM STRIKE

**HAITO UCHI**
RIDGE HAND STRIKE

**EMPI UCHI**
ELBOW STRIKE

TETTSUI UCHI - HAMMER FIST

MY TRADITIONAL KARATE PATHWAY
# STRENGTH, SKILL AND KNOWLEDGE

# ZUKI & UCHI WAZA

# MY NOTES & KEY POINTS

Attach your notes, pictures, scribble or write something important you've learned here.

MY TRADITIONAL KARATE PATHWAY
# STRENGTH, SKILL AND KNOWLEDGE

 # GERI WAZA - KICKS

Karate has very high emphasis on 'grounded' stability and balance for the obvious reasons. This is highlighted and very important to understand with the kicking techniques. Poorly balanced or badly executed kicks have no use in martial arts or sports. They risk an injury and will place you in disadvantage with any opponent, in any situation.

When learning and practising your kicks, learn to move, control, and complete a full kicking technique in a slow-motion without losing your balance, and keep in mind that 'High' in a kick does not equal effective. Start from lower level kicks and work your way up slowly as you get stronger, gain more control, and master the technique. Controlled repetition is the best way to develop correct muscles and muscle groups that are needed to support the techniques and able you to deliver effective kicks.

Don't try to short-cut your way into higher kicks by forcing them with speed and momentum, this will likely result in an injury and will only result in ineffective, poorly executed, and technically wrong kicks. To be able to perform and deliver a powerful and effective kick takes time and lots of practise. In the end, the hard work will pay off. Keep in mind that using correct techniques will allow anyone within 'average range of flexibility to learn, perform and deliver these kicks effectively.

MY TRADITIONAL KARATE PATHWAY
# STRENGTH, SKILL AND KNOWLEDGE

# GERI WAZA - KICKS

## MAE-GERI
FRONT KICK.

Extremely fast straight forward snap-kick with the ball of the foot (Koshi). Delivered either with your back or the front foot (Kizame-Geri). Maintain your height, keep your shoulders and hips squared to front and elbows close to your body. Keep the supporting foot firmly anchored to the ground with its toes pointing forward or slightly outwards. 'Slingshot' the kick in a straight line from the floor to the target by first raising your fully bent knee high up and pointed towards the target. Then 'together with thrusting your hips forward, slingshot the ball of the foot in an explosive, straight motion to the target. And, as quickly, snap it back. (Keep your toes curled back on the kicking foot).

Condition your leg muscles by standing in Heisoku Dachi with slightly bent knees and bring a bent knee as high up to your chest as you can without leaning or tilting your head forward. Repeat up and down ten times each side. Then lift your knee up and hold it there for as long as you can. (1 minute is a good target). Repeat with the other leg.

Just holding your leg up and keeping it still will strengthen the correct muscles you need to perform and control the kicks. Once you've gained enough strength, you can try this with a straight leg raised in a front of you.

MAE GERI

MY TRADITIONAL KARATE PATHWAY
STRENGTH, SKILL AND KNOWLEDGE

# GERI WAZA - KICKS

## YOKO-GERI-KEAGE

SIDE SNAP KICK (UPWARD MOTION).

Uses the outer side of the foot (Sokuto). Start by transferring your weight to one foot and standing (balanced) on it with a bent knee. Keep your weight low and the knee bent to allow adequate hip and joint movement.

Point your kicking leg's knee (Hiza) to your side, towards the target and bring it up to your side by brushing your foot up against the supporting leg. Rest the foot with its toes pointing down, on the supporting knee and keep the raised knee pointed at the target.

Then, rock and thrust your hips towards the target on your side and slingshot the outer side of the foot upwards in a circular motion to the target (E.g. Under the chin) and as quickly snap it back. (Don't allow the toes of the kicking foot to rise above the heel).

With the Keage, you will need to use your hips and legs together effectively. Exercise them together by standing (balanced) on one foot with a slightly bent knee. (Do not try to kick when standing on a straight leg). Lift and point your knee up to your side, rest its foot on the supporting knee. From here, keep the knee up and rock your hips open to your side and back. Repeat 10 times.

Next do this with slowly extending your leg and foot (heel above toes) directly to your side.

YOKO GERI KEAGE

MY TRADITIONAL KARATE PATHWAY
# STRENGTH, SKILL AND KNOWLEDGE

# GERI WAZA - KICKS

## YOKO-GERI-KEKOMI
SIDE THRUST KICK (IN STRAIGHT LINE)

One of the most powerful kicks in Martial Arts. Delivered with the heel or the bottom of your foot. Imagine stomping and breaking a branch of a tree that is lying on the ground but, doing it sideways.

Stand in a Horse-riding stance (Kiba Dachi) and maintain your height and knee angle. Bring a bent knee high up to your chest in a centre of your gravity. Then pivot your supporting foot and hips around to bring the chambered leg and the knee in a horizontal plane at your belt level with the bottom of your foot (and your behind) now aimed directly at the target. From here, extend and 'thrust' your foot in one straight explosive motion to the target. (Imagine breaking that branch). And as quickly snap it back.

Practise and condition your leg muscles by standing in a Heisoku Dachi and bring your straight leg up to your side, close to a 45-degree angle. Then swing it up and down around ten times. Next hold the leg up for as long as you can. (1 minute is a good target). Then repeat with the other leg

Just holding your leg up and keeping it still will strengthen the correct muscles you need to perform and control the kicks.

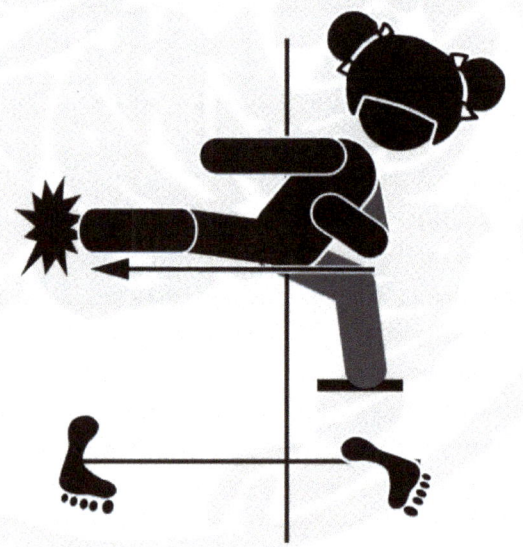

YOKO GERI KEKOMI

MY TRADITIONAL KARATE PATHWAY
STRENGTH, SKILL AND KNOWLEDGE

# GERI WAZA - KICKS

## MAWASHI - GERI

ROUND HOUSE KICK (front or back foot).

Fast and powerful 'circular kick' using hips, body rotation, and a 'slingshot' motion to generate speed and power. This kick is done either with the ball, or with top of the foot. (The top of the foot is used in sparring and competitions for safety reasons).

In a front stance, bring your bent back knee high up from the side and transfer your weight and your centre of gravity to the front foot. Imagine lifting your knee to mount a bicycle. Maintain your balance, front knee angle, and keep your kicking leg chambered. Then, in one motion, leading with the bent knee, use the gained speed, momentum, and your hips to pivot around your supporting foot to bring your hips sideways to the target and the bent knee to the front. Keep the knee aimed at the target. From here, without stopping, 'slingshot' the foot from your bent leg in a 'hay cutting' motion to the target. And as quickly, snap it back. (Ensure your knee does not travel past the target).

Best exercise to condition your muscles and improve your balance in Mawashi Geri is to repeat the entire technique in a slow motion. (without shortcutting the moves or losing your balance). Hold your leg up as long as you can, then bring it slowly back in a controlled fashion.

MAWASHI GERI

MY TRADITIONAL KARATE PATHWAY
# STRENGTH, SKILL AND KNOWLEDGE

# GERI WAZA - KICKS

### USHIRO - GERI
**BACKWARDS KICK**

Another powerful kick. Imagine kicking backwards with your heel like a horse. To start, stand in a front stance. Bring your front knee in, up and close to your body. Transfer your weight and centre of your gravity on your back foot. Then thrust and drive your heel (toes down) straight backwards in an explosive motion directly to the target behind you. And as quickly, snap it back.

Best exercise to condition your muscles for Ushiro Geri is to repeat the entire technique in a slow motion (without losing your balance) and hold your leg up as long as you can then bring it slowly back in a controlled fashion.

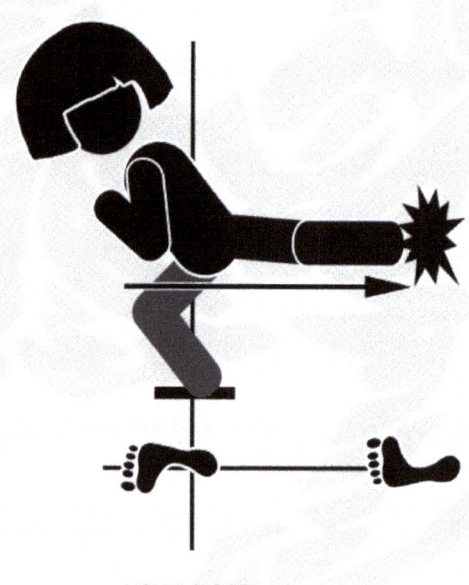

USHIRO GERI

MY TRADITIONAL KARATE PATHWAY
STRENGTH, SKILL AND KNOWLEDGE

# GERI WAZA - KICKS

### FUMIKOMI - GERI
STOMP KICK

Stomping kick, the name says it all. Imagine breaking a branch of a tree that is lying on the ground. Lift your knee up and stomp your flat foot or the heel to crush the target.

FUMIKOMI - GERI

Worth to research: Mikazuki-Geri, Hiza-Geri, Nami-Gaeshi, Ura-Mawashi-Geri, Ashi Barai and Mae-Tobi-Geri.

MY TRADITIONAL KARATE PATHWAY
# STRENGTH, SKILL AND KNOWLEDGE

# GERI WAZA
## MY NOTES & KEY POINTS

Attach your notes, pictures, scribble or write something important you've learned here.

MY TRADITIONAL KARATE PATHWAY
# STRENGTH, SKILL AND KNOWLEDGE

# UKE WAZA - BLOCKS

Uke derives from a Japanese word 'Ukeru' to receive. In Karate we can use our 'blocking' techniques to our advantage in multiple ways in order to protect ourselves from harm.

Commonly in defence, to 'receive', that is to deflect, divert or catch a punch or a kick, and to change our position from disadvantage to advantage one. We also use those same techniques to clear path, catch, grapple, break or strike, and as precursors to our counter strikes in short combination techniques (Renzoku-Waza).

As with the other techniques, to be effective, you must learn to use them together with your hips, (Koshi-Waza), stance techniques (Dachi-Waza) and footwork (Ashi-Waza).

SOTO-UKE

MY TRADITIONAL KARATE PATHWAY
# STRENGTH, SKILL AND KNOWLEDGE

# UKE WAZA - BLOCKS

Uke derives from Japanese word 'to receive'.

## GEDAN BARAI

Lower (Sweep) Block

A lower 'sweeping' block. To defend against lower body attacks at Gedan-level. To start, bring your right fist up to your left ear (brush it up across your chest) palm side facing the ear. Ensure your elbow has travelled past the centreline of your chest. Now, point your (straight) left arm to the 'target'. From here, together with the Hikite, and your hips opening to Hanmi, leading with the back of the fist, sweep the fist down along the left arm and in a circular motion, fully extend it above your front knee. Fist should end up knuckles up, directly above the front knee and aligned with the knee and the shoulder. Receive the attack with the flat outer wrist, back fist, or back of your forearm (not with the side bone) and deflect it by rotating/ snapping the wrist and forearm around. (Back of the fist ends facing up). When blocking, receive and deflect, do not hit.

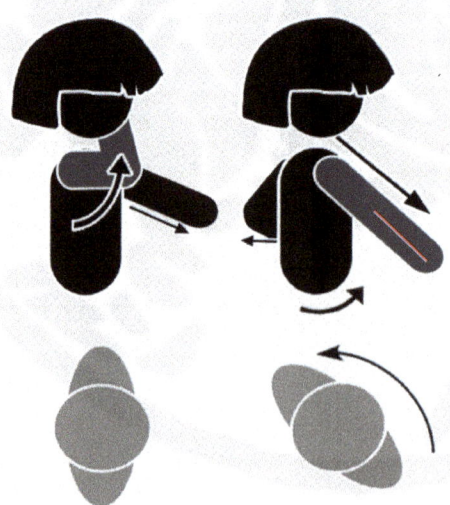

GEDAN-BARAI

MY TRADITIONAL KARATE PATHWAY
# STRENGTH, SKILL AND KNOWLEDGE

 # UKE WAZA - BLOCKS

## AGE-UKE

'RISING' OR 'UPPER' BLOCK.

To defend against higher level attacks aimed at the head (Jodan level).

Start with the fist on your side (from Hikite position). Brush it straight up across the centre-front of your chest with its palm facing in. Once your fist reaches the Jodan level (just under the chin), bring the upper-arm up across your face in a 45 degree angle, and level it, with the elbow, slightly above and in a front of your forehead (Hitae). (At next level, once blocked, open your blocking hand and capture the opponent's arm. Tsukami-Uke).

Elbow should end up aligned with the shoulder. 'Receive' the attack with the back of your forearm or your wrist while in upwards motion and deflect it by rotating your wrist and forearm around (Inner-upper-arm to front). Leave a gap (A fist width) between the forearm and your forehead and don't block your view either to the front or to the side with your arm.

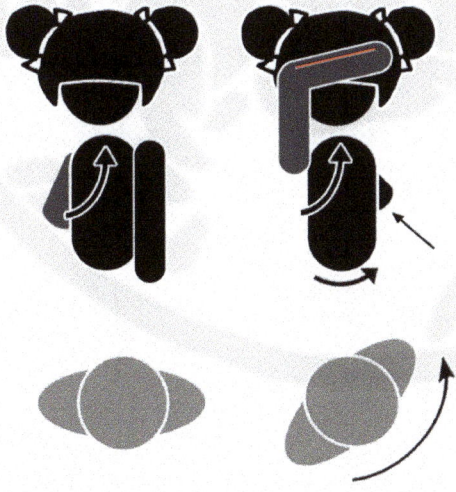

AGE-UKE

MY TRADITIONAL KARATE PATHWAY
STRENGTH, SKILL AND KNOWLEDGE

# UKE WAZA - BLOCKS

## UCHI-UKE
INSIDE BLOCK

From 'inside - out' motion block. Mainly used to protect your body from attacks at 'Chudan' level. To start, stand with your hips squared to front (in 'Shomen') and bring your blocking forearm horizontally across your lower chest with the back of your fist facing up. (Keep your elbow stationary during the block). At the same time, straighten your other arm above it and in a front of you, and point it to the target at Chudan level.

Then, simultaneously with the opposite hip rotation (to 'Hanmi') and 'Hikite', swing the right forearm around its elbow to upright position directly in a front of your shoulder, and rotate the back of the fist to face forward. Elbow should be pointing down, aligned with the shoulder, and bent at 90 degrees. Your fist should be at the shoulder level, knuckles to front. Receive the attack with flat outer wrist or back of your forearm (not the side bone) and deflect it by rotating/ flipping the wrist and forearm around. Receive and deflect, do not hit.

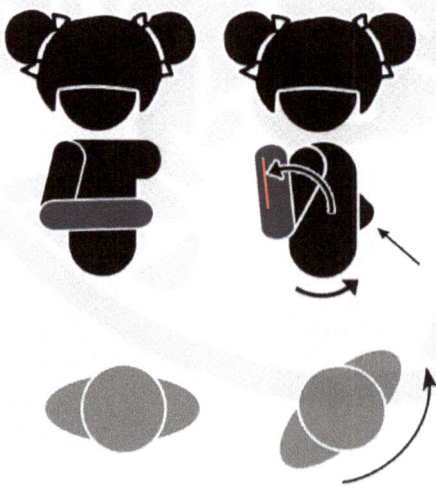

UCHI-UKE

MY TRADITIONAL KARATE PATHWAY
# STRENGTH, SKILL AND KNOWLEDGE

# UKE WAZA - BLOCKS

## SOTO-UKE

**OUTSIDE BLOCK**

From 'outside-in' block. Like the Uchi-Uke, mainly used to protect your body from attacks at 'Chudan' level. Start, with your hips and shoulders squared to front. Bring your clenched fist up to your side with the palm and inner arm facing outwards, elbow at the shoulder level in a 90-degree angle. At the same time, straighten your other arm in a front of you and point it to the target at Chudan level.

Then, together with the 'Hikite', in a circular motion, with your hips and shoulders, bring the bent arm (palm first), directly in a front you and rotate the wrist around to bring the back of your fist to the front. Fist should end up aligned with the shoulder, at the shoulder height, elbow pointing down and bent at 90 degrees. Receive the attack with your inner wrist or inner arm and deflect it by rotating/ flipping the wrist and forearm around. Receive and deflect, do not hit.

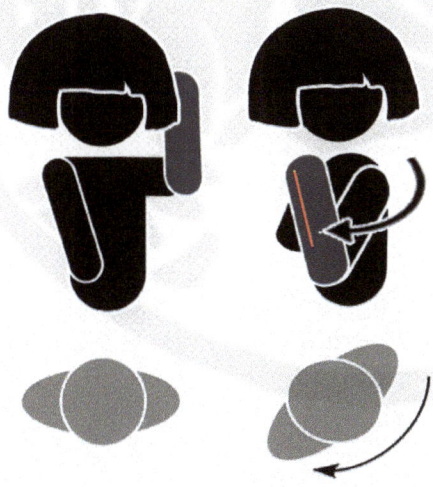

SOTO-UKE

MY TRADITIONAL KARATE PATHWAY
STRENGTH, SKILL AND KNOWLEDGE

# UKE WAZA - BLOCKS

## SHUTO-UKE

**KNIFE HAND BLOCK**

Bring your (open) right hand up to your left ear with the palm facing the ear. (Brush it up across your chest). Ensure your elbow has travelled past the centreline of your chest. At the same time, straighten your left arm in a front of you and point it to the target at Chudan level.

From here, leading with the thumb side (Haito) sweep the back of your right hand down along the top of your left arm. Once your right hand reaches the left elbow, together with the 'Hikite' and rotating your hips open to Hanmi, sweep your hand to the right side (In a front of your shoulder) and rotate the hand around its wrist to 'Shuto'.

Your elbow and hand should end up aligned and in a front of your shoulder with fingertips at the shoulder level, elbow pointing down and bent at 90 degrees. Receive the attack with the thumb-side or the back-hand side of the wrist and deflect it by rotating/ snapping the wrist and hand around to Shuto.

SHUTO-UKE

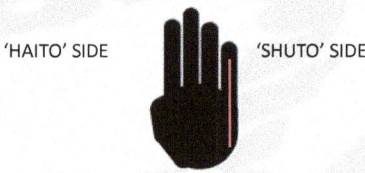

'HAITO' SIDE       'SHUTO' SIDE

MY TRADITIONAL KARATE PATHWAY
STRENGTH, SKILL AND KNOWLEDGE

# UKE WAZA

## MY NOTES & KEY POINTS

Attach your notes, pictures, scribble or write something important you've learned here.

MY TRADITIONAL KARATE PATHWAY
# STRENGTH, SKILL AND KNOWLEDGE

# KUMITE - SPARRING

One and Five-Step kumite drills are a 'controlled simulated fighting environment' where we test, practise, develop and improve our (Kihon) skills and techniques against a real person and learn to adjust, manipulate, and control the critical aspects of our defences and offences (Balance, Distance, Timing and Accuracy) in a real time. The Jiyu-Ippon (Semi-free) and the Jiyu (Free) kumite are for pressure testing and improving those skills on a higher level.

## TARGET LEVELS

For the purpose of the exercise, clarity and safety, we inform our training partners clearly on our intended target levels and techniques. This will allow our partners to prepare and fully focus on learning the right technique.

**'JODAN'** –   UPPER LEVEL
Level above the neck.  (Jodan punch, blocked with Age-Uke).

**'CHUDAN** - MID LEVEL
Level above the belt. (Chudan Punch, blocked with Soto-Uke or Uchi Uke).

**'GEDAN**    LOWER LEVEL
Under the waist level.  (Mae-Geri blocked with Gedan-Barai).

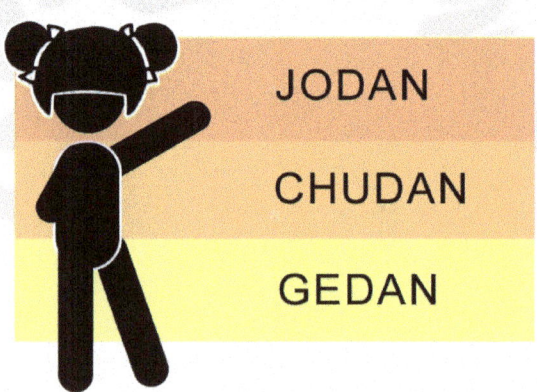

MY TRADITIONAL KARATE PATHWAY
# STRENGTH, SKILL AND KNOWLEDGE

# KUMITE - SPARRING

## IPPON KUMITE
ONE STEP SPARRING DRILL WITH A PARTNER

Sensei will set up your routine and determine what techniques are practised and in what order. You will line up, face, and greet your partner by bowing in Musubi Dachi and take a Heiko Dachi ready stance ('YOI').

The person attacking starts by stepping back into Zenkutsu Dachi at striking distance. They clearly inform their partner of the technique they are going to use and their intended 'target', (Jodan punch, chudan punch, or a kick). Then with a forward step, deliver their technique (Punch or Kick) as close to the target (E.g. Face) as is considered safe and requirement at their belt grade. When stepping forward, move in a straight line and try to step near or next to the 'insole' of your partner's front foot. (Not on their toes!). It is important to deliver your punch (or kick) with an intent to reach the target. Otherwise, the opportunity to learn will be lost for both of you.

Person defending will response to the attack by stepping back into relevant defensive stance (E.g. Zenkutsu Dachi) and using relevant defensive technique (E.g. Age-Uke) to block the attack, then perform a counter strike with 'Kiai'. (E.g. Gyaku Zuki). When stepping backwards you will need to step far enough to avoid the punch but, stay close enough (at striking distance) to be able to deliver a counter strike.

Once the drill is over, or when you change partners, you should thank your current partner (and welcome the new one) with a bow.

*Continue...*

MY TRADITIONAL KARATE PATHWAY
# STRENGTH, SKILL AND KNOWLEDGE

# KUMITE - SPARRING

## IPPON KUMITE Continued...

When moving backwards, pay extra attention where and how you place your back foot. How far and how wide will determine how effectively you can block, counter strike, maintain your balance or move again.

MY TRADITIONAL KARATE PATHWAY
# STRENGTH, SKILL AND KNOWLEDGE

# KUMITE - SPARRING

## GOHON KUMITE

5-STEP SPARRING DRILL WITH A PARTNER.

In five-step sparring you work exactly as in Ippon Kumite, but the person attacking will deliver the same technique consecutively 5 times in a row stepping forward each time, and 'Kiai' only on the last one. The Person defending will response and step backwards in a straight line for those 5 times and only deliver the counter strike with 'Kiai' on the last one. Then, you will reverse your roles and work your way back to the start.

## JIYU IPPON KUMITE

SEMI-FREE ONE-STEP SPARRING WITH A PARTNER

As in 'Ippon Kumite' with the set techniques, 'one strike and one response' at the time, but both 'opponents' (training partners) are moving freely in their 'Kamae' (fighting stance) and deliver their techniques and respond to attacks in 'real time' in more realistic scenario. Purpose of this training is to condition ourselves (mentally and physically), and to adjust our speed, balance, accuracy, and distance to work in real-life scenarios and in competition environment. Next level up from here is **JIYU Kumite**, free fighting kumite with no set techniques or any advanced notice for techniques used.

MY TRADITIONAL KARATE PATHWAY

# STRENGTH, SKILL AND KNOWLEDGE

# KUMITE

## MY NOTES & KEY POINTS

Attach your notes, pictures, scribble or write something important you've learned here.

MY TRADITIONAL KARATE PATHWAY
STRENGTH, SKILL AND KNOWLEDGE

# KATA - PATTERNS

## Purpose of Kata

'Katas' are one of the three main pillars of Karate learning. Kihon, Kata and Kumite.

Katas combine our stances and footwork with other techniques and places them in a predetermined 'Fight-Simulation' where the imagined 'threats', their direction, nature and required 'responses' changes almost with each step taken. Lower-level Katas start with the basic moves but, are by no means, less effective (rather the opposite) than the higher-level Katas that require much more experience, technical skills and further knowledge to perform correctly.

With Kata, we practise shifting our focus and direction, learn to control our timing, practise quick and slow movements, shift from extreme acceleration to fully controlled stops. We move from high jumps to 'slow-motion' techniques. We learn stability and balancing in high and low stances. We learn to deliver powerful and explosive techniques with **\*Kime'**. Katas provide us a platform and a practise ground for vast number of variations and combinations that strengthen, condition and improve our mental and physical abilities to response effectively in variable situations. Katas are also used as a 'benchmark' and a tool to test, review, and showcase our skill levels and abilities.

When you get on that floor to perform your Kata, do your best, thrive to your best performance every time but, don't hold back because you are afraid of making a mistake or afraid to fail. Mistakes do happen, we learn from them, they make us work harder and in the end, they make us better and stronger. Take your strongest ready stance, put your warrior face on and have a go at it.

MY TRADITIONAL KARATE PATHWAY
# STRENGTH, SKILL AND KNOWLEDGE

# KATA - PATTERNS

## Performing Kata

Walk in a centre front of the mat, face the front and bow to the front. Hold your head high, eyes up and walk confidently on the mat, directly to your starting spot, and take a Musubi Dachi stance. Next, make a calm and respectful bow to the front, stand up and strongly shout out your Kata name. Then take a confident 'Yoi' stance (Heiko Dachi) and start the kata moves. At the end, after your last move, retract in a strong and controlled fashion back to your 'Yoi' stance facing the front again. Take a Musubi Dachi stance, bow and retract out from the mat

- Kata starts and ends with a bow (Rei).
- Kata starts and finishes at the same exact spot.
- The first move in each kata is a block, ("There is no first strike in Karate").

Always keep an upright posture and maintain your head height throughout the Kata, unless a specific technique requires you to do something else, like jumping or kneeling etc. Pay attention to your breathing, its timing and rhythm and ensure your slow and fast movements are clearly distinguishable as 'slow' and 'fast'. Ensure the fast and quick moves are complete, don't shortcut a move to be quicker or faster. When performing a move or a technique, do it with its 'real intent' and pay extra attention your the balance.

Learn and understand your Katas. Katas are not just for a show. Think, what is the main purpose of your Kata? What is the real intent of each technique? How can I make them effective in a real life scenario? This will help you to remember and perform your kata much better.

Know your Kata, when you don't, it shows.

MY TRADITIONAL KARATE PATHWAY
STRENGTH, SKILL AND KNOWLEDGE

# KATA - PATTERNS

## Our recommended order of learning Katas. (By belt colours/ Kyu level)

| | | | |
|---|---|---|---|
| TAIKYOKU SHODAN | LEARN | KNOW | 10-9 Kyu |
| JO NO | LEARN | KNOW | 9-8 Kyu |
| | | | |
| HEIAN SHODAN | LEARN | KNOW | 9-8 Kyu |
| HEIAN NIDAN | LEARN | KNOW | 8-7 Kyu |
| HEIAN SANDAN | LEARN | KNOW | 7-6 Kyu |
| HEIAN YONDAN | LEARN | KNOW | 6-5 Kyu |
| HEIAN GODAN | LEARN | KNOW | 5-4 Kyu |
| | | | |
| TEKKI SHODAN | LEARN | KNOW | 4-3 Kyu |
| | | | |
| BASSAI DAI | LEARN | KNOW | 3-1 Kyu to 1 Dan |
| JION | LEARN | KNOW | 3-1 Kyu to 1 Dan |
| EMPI | LEARN | KNOW | 3-1 Kyu to 1 Dan |
| KANKU DAI | LEARN | KNOW | 3-1 Kyu to 1 Dan |

**\*KIME!** A focus point. The moment of a controlled delivery and completion of any Karate technique to its maximum impact and power. The Muscle 'power' contraction point, 'Relaxed, Contracted, Relaxed'. the "100" of "0-100-0".

**\*KIAI!** Is the name of our 'battle cry' or a short 'shout out', to assist us releasing the full power of our 'Kime' in our Kihon, Kata and Kumite training. We are not actually saying 'Kiai. Have a go, don't hold back and try it with your punch! (Hi-yah!, Aiyah!, Eeee-yah! or Hyah!').

MY TRADITIONAL KARATE PATHWAY
# STRENGTH, SKILL AND KNOWLEDGE

# KATA-PATTERNS

## KEY POINTS IN KATA PERFORMANCE

- **Stances** - Size, foot positioning, knee and foot angles and orientation, weight distribution, balance, stability, height, and posture.
- **Techniques**' – Correct, complete, effective for their intended purpose and target, speed, distance, accuracy, strength and 'kime'
- **Transitional movements** – Control, balance, stability, weight transfer and distribution, speed, height, posture and foot position.
- **Timing** – Correct rhythm and flow with clearly completed techniques, transitions and stops. Clear distinction between the slow and fast movements. The total time taken to finish.
- **Breathing** – Correct breathing technique. Timing of inhaling/ out haling when completing a technique.
- **Focus** (KIME) – Strength and ability to control and deliver techniques with Kime 0-100-0.
- Using the **actual movements** as intended in the kata.

- **Strength**
- **Speed**
- **Balance**
- **Knowledge** – Know your Kata. Have a clear idea and intention for the moves you perform, when you don't, it shows.

## EMBUSEN
The 'shape' or the 'path' Kata follows

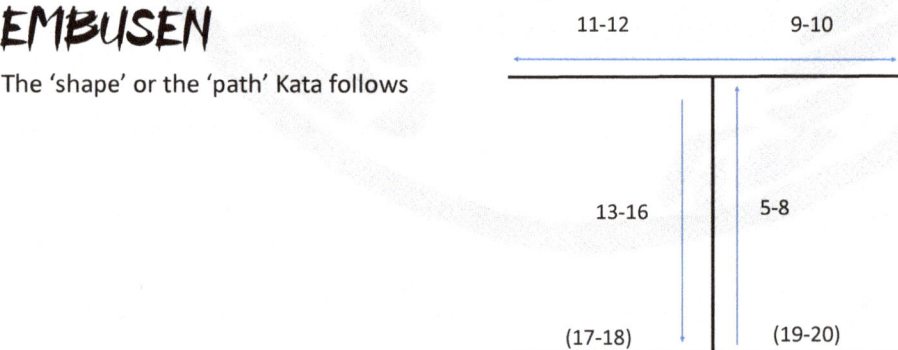

MY TRADITIONAL KARATE PATHWAY
STRENGTH, SKILL AND KNOWLEDGE

# KATA

## MY KATA LEARNING PLAN

- [ ] TAIKYOKU SHODAN
- [ ] JO NO
- [ ] HEIAN SHODAN
- [ ] HEIAN NIDAN
- [ ] HEIAN SANDAN
- [ ] HEIAN YONDAN
- [ ] HEIAN GODAN
- [ ] TEKKI SHODAN

- [ ] BASSAI DAI
- [ ] EMPI
- [ ] JION
- [ ] KANKU DAI

MY TRADITIONAL KARATE PATHWAY
# STRENGTH, SKILL AND KNOWLEDGE

# TAIKYOKU SHODAN

The 'Ultimate First' Kata

Our first and most basic Kata with only two basic moves in it. The Lower Block and Trough Punch, (Gedan Barai + Oi-Zuki). In total it has twenty moves, which are all performed in a front stance (Zenkutsu Dachi). We Learn to use our 90° Left-Turns, 180° Right D-Turns, and 270° Around the back-Turns to the left. All the turns lead to down block (Gedan Barai) and all the forward steps are performed with the 'step through' punch, (Oi-zuki).

| | |
|---|---|
| Name | **TAIKYOKU SHODAN – 'ULTIMATE FIRST LEVEL'** |
| Moves | 20 |
| KIAI | 8 & 16 |
| Techniques | Lower block (GEDAN BARAI), Through Punch (OI-ZUKI) |
| Stances | Zenkutsu Dachi |

## EMBUSEN
The 'shape' or the 'path' Kata follows

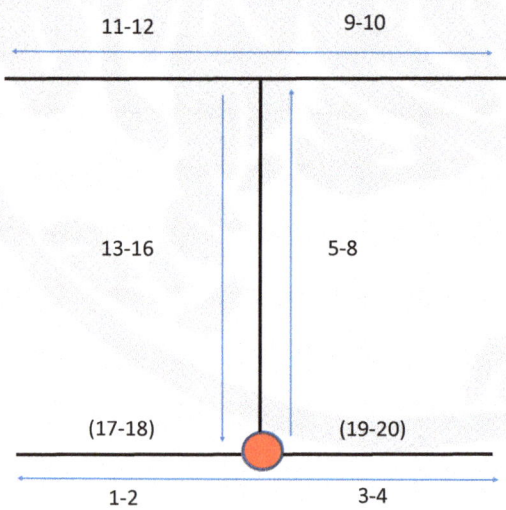

MY TRADITIONAL KARATE PATHWAY

# STRENGTH, SKILL AND KNOWLEDGE

# TAIKYOKU SHODAN

 90° LH

 180° RH

 90° LH

 270° LH

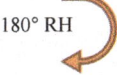 180° RH

 90° LH

 270° LH

 180° RH

1.  LH GEDAN BARAI / LH ZENKUTSU DACHI
2.  RH CHUDAN OI-ZUKI / RH ZENKUTSU DACHI
3.  RH GEDAN BARAI / RH ZENKUTSU DACHI
4.  LH CHUDAN OI-ZUKI / LH ZENKUTSU DACHI — KIAI !!!
5.  LH GEDAN BARAI / LH ZENKUTSU DACHI
6.  RH / RH
7. + LH / + LH
8.  + RH CHUDAN OI-ZUKI / + RH ZENKUTSU DACHI
9.  LH GEDAN BARAI / LH ZENKUTSU DACHI
10.  RH CHUDAN OI-ZUKI / RH ZENKUTSU DACHI
11.  RH GEDAN BARAI / RH ZENKUTSU DACHI
12.  LH CHUDAN OI-ZUKI / LH ZENKUTSU DACHI — KIAI !!!
13.  LH GEDAN BARAI / LH ZENKUTSU DACHI
14.  RH / RH
15. + LH / + LH
16.  + RH OI-ZUKI / + RH ZENKUTSU DACHI
17.  LH GEDAN BARAI / LH ZENKUTSU DACHI
18.  RH CHUDAN OI-ZUKI / RH ZENKUTSU DACHI
19.  RH GEDAN BARAI / RH ZENKUTSU DACHI
20.  LH CHUDAN OI-ZUKI / LH ZENKUTSU DACHI

MY TRADITIONAL KARATE PATHWAY
# STRENGTH, SKILL AND KNOWLEDGE

# JO NO

Our second Kata introduces us Jodan and Chudan level blocking with Age-Uke and Soto-Uke. It also introduces us the front kick, Mae-Geri, and the two Knife-hand blocks Shuto-Uke and Tate-Shuto-Uke (Vertical Knife-hand block). When performing steps 17-19, pay extra attention to how you transition your centre of gravity between the stances, and make sure you have clearly distinguishable 'slow and fast' moves.

| | |
|---|---|
| **Name** | JO NO |
| **Moves** | 21 |
| **KIAI** | 8 & 21 |
| **Techniques** | Lower block (Gedan Barai), Upper Block (Age-Uke), Through Punch (Oi-Zuki), Outer Block (Soto-Uke), Front Kick (Mae-Geri), Knife Hand Block (Shuto-Uke), (Vertical) Tate-Shuto-Uke, Front Punch (Choku-Zuki). |
| **Stances** | Zenkutsu Dachi, Kokutsu Dachi, Kiba Dachi |

## EMBUSEN
The 'shape' or the 'path' Kata follows

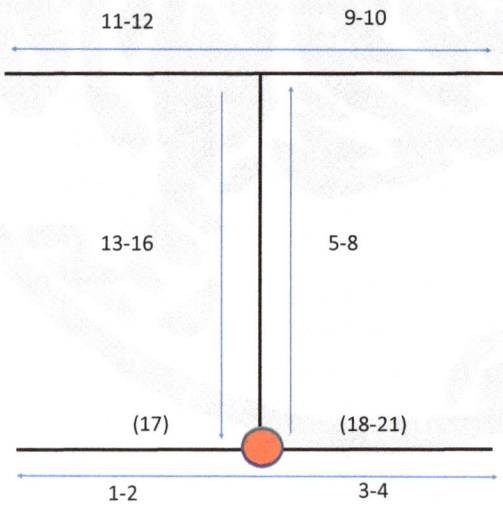

# MY TRADITIONAL KARATE PATHWAY
## STRENGTH, SKILL AND KNOWLEDGE

型 JO NO

| | | | |
|---|---|---|---|
| HIDARI 90° LH | **1** LH GEDAN BARAI / LH ZENKUTSU DACHI | **2** RH AGE-UKE / RH ZENKUTSU DACHI | |
| 180° RH | **3** RH GEDAN BARAI / RH ZENKUTSU DACHI | **4** LH AGE-UKE / LH ZENKUTSU DACHI — KIAI!!! | |
| 90° LH | **5** LH GEDAN BARAI / LH ZENKUTSU DACHI | **6** RH / RH | **7** + LH / + LH | **8** + RH CHUDAN OI-ZUKI / + RH ZENKUTSU DACHI |
| 270° LH | **9** LH GEDAN BARAI / LH ZENKUTSU DACHI | **10** RH SOTO-UKE / RH ZENKUTSU DACHI | |
| 180° RH | **11** RH GEDAN BARAI / RH ZENKUTSU DACHI | **12** LH SOTO-UKE / LH ZENKUTSU DACHI | |
| 90° LH | **13** TWO HAND GEDAN BARAI / LH ZENKUTSU DACHI | **14** RH / RH | **15** + LH / + LH | **16** + RH MAE-GERI / + RH ZENKUTSU DACHI |
| 270° LH | **17** LH SHUTO-UKE / RH KOKUTSU DACHI | | | |
| 180° RH | **18** RH SHUTO-UKE / LH KOKUTSU DACHI | **19** RH TATE-SHUTO-UKE / KIBA DACHI | **20 21** LH + RH CHOKU-ZUKI COMBO / KIBA DACHI — KIAI!!! |

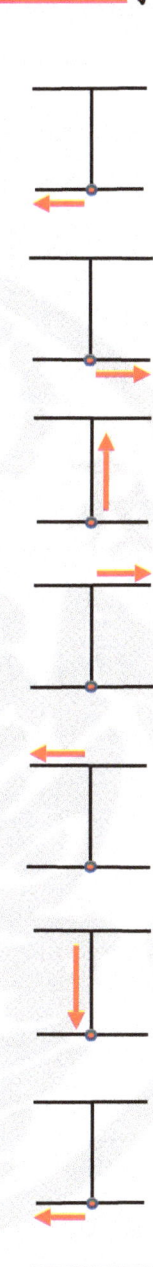

MY TRADITIONAL KARATE PATHWAY
# STRENGTH, SKILL AND KNOWLEDGE

 # HEIAN SHODAN

First of the five Heian 'The Peaceful Mind' Katas with twenty one moves. It introduces us to Gedan-Barai, Oi-Zuki, Tettsui Uchi ('Hammer fist Strike'), and Age-Uke performed in Zenkutsu Dachi, and to Shuto-Uke performed in Kokutsu-Dachi with 180, 90 and 45 degree turns.

| | |
|---|---|
| **Name** | **HEIAN SHODAN,** 'THE PEACEFUL MIND' FIRST LEVEL |
| **Moves** | 21 |
| **KIAI** | 9 & 17 |
| **Techniques** | Lower block (Gedan Barai), Through Punch (Oi-Zuki), Hammer Fist Strike (Tettsui-Uchi), Upper Block (Age-Uke), Knife Hand Block (Shuto-Uke) |
| **Stances** | Zenkutsu Dachi, Kokutsu Dachi. |

## EMBUSEN
The 'shape' or the 'path' Kata follows

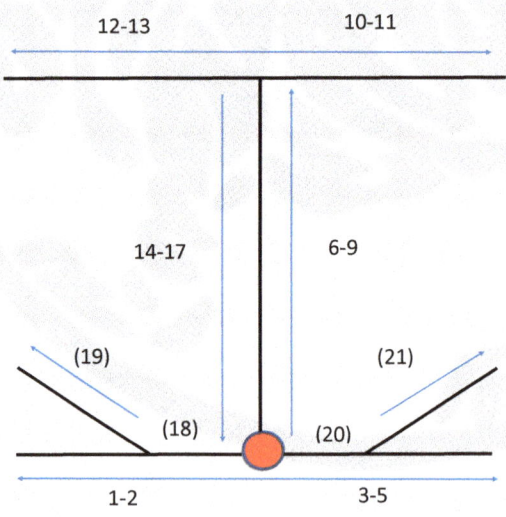

MY TRADITIONAL KARATE PATHWAY
# STRENGTH, SKILL AND KNOWLEDGE

# 型 HEIAN SHODAN

| Turn | # | Technique |
|---|---|---|
| 90° LH | 1 | LH GEDAN BARAI / LH ZENKUTSU DACHI |
|  | 2 | RH CHUDAN OI-ZUKI / RH ZENKUTSU DACHI |
| 180° RH | 3 | RH GEDAN BARAI / RH ZENKUTSU DACHI |
|  | 4 | RH TETTSUI UCHI / RH SHO-ZENKUTSU |
| 90° LH | 5 | LH CHUDAN OI-ZUKI / LH ZENKUTSU DACHI — KIAI!!! |
|  | 6 | LH GEDAN BARAI / LH ZENKUTSU DACHI |
|  | 7 | RH / RH |
|  | 8 | + LH / + LH |
|  | 9 | + RH AGE-UKE / + RH ZENKUTSU DACHI |
| 270° LH | 10 | LH GEDAN BARAI / LH ZENKUTSU DACHI |
|  | 11 | RH CHUDAN OI-ZUKI / RH ZENKUTSU DACHI |
| 180° RH | 12 | RH GEDAN BARAI / RH ZENKUTSU DACHI |
|  | 13 | LH CHUDAN OI-ZUKI / LH ZENKUTSU DACHI |
| 90° LH | 14 | LH GEDAN BARAI / LH ZENKUTSU DACHI |
|  | 15 | RH / RH |
|  | 16 | + LH / + LH |
|  | 17 | + RH OI-ZUKI / + RH ZENKUTSU DACHI — KIAI!!! |
| 270° LH | 18 | LH SHUTO-UKE / RH KOKUTSU DACHI |
| 45° RH | 19 | RH SHUTO-UKE / LH KOKUTSU DACHI |
| 180° RH | 20 | RH SHUTO-UKE / LH KOKUTSU DACHI |
| 45° LH | 21 | HH SHUTO-UKE / RH KOKUTSU DACHI |

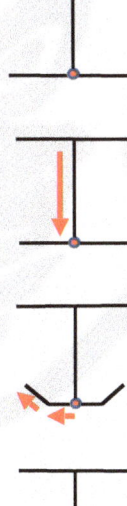

MY TRADITIONAL KARATE PATHWAY
STRENGTH, SKILL AND KNOWLEDGE

 # KATA

## MY NOTES & KEY POINTS

Attach your notes, pictures, or scribble something important you've learned here.

# KARATE VOCABULARY

**Common Words**
Back - Ura
Basics – Kihon
Begin – Hajime
Behind– Ushiro
Belt– Obi
Black Belt Rank – Dan
Bow – Rei
Color Belt Rank – Kyu
Fist – Ken
Focus – Kime
Foot – Ashi
Forward - Mae
Kick – Geri
Kneeling– Seiza
Left – Hidari
Line Up – Seiretsu
Lower Level – Gedan
Main Instructor – Sensei
Meditate – Mokuso
Middle (Stomach Level) – Chudan
Punching Board – Makiwara
Right – Migi
School (Martial Arts) – Dojo
Senior Student/ Instructor – Sempai
Sokumen – Side
Sparring – Kumite
Stance – Dachi
Start - Hajime
Stop – Yame

Shifting - Tai Sabaki  (from attack line)
Technique – Waza
To the side - Yoko
Turn Around – Mawatte
Uniform – Gi (Gee)
Upper (Head Level) – Jodan

**Stances – (DACHI)**
Back Stance – Kokutsu Dachi
Cat Stance – Neko Ashi Dachi
Crane Stance - Tsuru Ashi Dashi
Crossed Feet Stance – Kosa Dachi
Feet Together – Heisoku Dachi
Feet V Shape – Musubi Dachi
Front Stance – Zenkutsu Dachi
Horse Riding Stance – Kiba Dachi
Immovable Stance – Fudo Dachi
Knee bending - Hizakutsu Dachi
Leg Stance- Ashi Dachi
L Stance – Renoji Dachi
Ready Stance – Heiko Dachi
T Stance – Teiji Dachi

# KARATE VOCABULARY

**Blocks – (UKE)**
Augmented Block – Morote Uke
Cross Hand Block – Juji Uke
Inside Block – Uchi Uke
Knife Hand Block – Shuto Uke
Lower Block – Gedan Barai
Outside Block – Soto Uke
Palm Block – Teisho Uke
Rising Block – Age Uke
Wedge Block - Kakiwake

**Punches (ZUKI) & Hand/Arm Strikes (UCHI)**
Back Fist Strike – Uraken Uchi
Elbow Strike – Empi Uchi
Front Punch – Choku Zuki
Hammer fist – Tettsui Uchi
Hook Punch – Kage Zuki
Knife Hand Strike – Shuto Uchi
Leading Punch – Kizame Zuki
Lunge Punch – Oi Zuki
Mountain Punch – Yama Zuki
Palm Heel Strike – Teisho Uchi
Reverse Punch – Gyaku Zuki
Ridge Hand Strike – Haito Uchi
Rising Punch – Age Zuki
Sanbon Zuki – 3 Punch Combination
Spear Hand Strike – Nukite

**Kicks – (GERI)**
Back Thrust Kick – Ushiro Geri
Crescent Kick – Mika Zuki Geri
Foot Sweep – Ashi Barai
Front Kick – Mae Geri
Knee Kick – Hiza Geri
Nami Gaeshi – Returning Wave
Roundhouse Kick – Mawashi Geri
Side Snap Kick – Yoko Geri Keage
Side Thrust Kick – Yoko Geri Kekomi
Stomp Kick – Fumikomi Geri

**Counting**
1 Ichi, 2 Ni, 3 San, 4 Shi, 5 Go,
6 Roku, 7 Sichi, 8 Hachi, 9 Ku, 10 Yu

MY TRADITIONAL KARATE PATHWAY
STRENGTH, SKILL AND KNOWLEDGE

# MOKYHUO - GOALS

### Doryoku No Seichin O Yashinau Koto

| MY GOALS AND TARGETS | ACHIEVED |
|---|---|
|  |  |
|  |  |
|  |  |
|  |  |
|  |  |
|  |  |
|  |  |
|  |  |
|  |  |
|  |  |
|  |  |
|  |  |
|  |  |
|  |  |
|  |  |
|  |  |
|  |  |

# NIJU KUN

## 20 Guiding Principles of Karate-DO

by Gichin Funakoshi

- Karate begins and ends with bowing (courtesy and respect).
- There is no first strike in karate, (Karate is for defence).
- Karate stands on a side of justice.
- First know yourself, then know the others.
- Cultivating mind is more important than learning a technique.
- Heart (mind) must be set free.
- Accidents come from carelessness.
- Karate training is not only for the Dojo
- Learning karate is a lifetime journey.
- The beauty in the Way of Karate, it can be applied to everything.
- Karate is like boiling water. If not heated, it will cool down.
- Do not think of winning. Instead, think of not losing.
- Assess and observe your opponent then adjust yourself accordingly
- The outcome of a fight, depends on one's ability to understand weaknesses and strengths
- Think of hands and feet as swords.
- Once you step beyond your own gate, you will face a million enemies.
- Formal stances are for beginners, expert moves naturally.
- Kata can be precise and perfectly performed, real fight is another thing.
- Do not forget the employment of withdrawal of power, the extension or contraction of the body, the swift or leisurely application of technique
- Keep on thinking, and seek new ways

MY TRADITIONAL KARATE PATHWAY
# STRENGTH, SKILL AND KNOWLEDGE

# MY KARATE JOURNEY

## MY 100 DAY JOURNAL

My important dates, events, key points from lessons and memories.

Date ___/___/_____

Date ___/___/_____

Date ___/___/_____

Date ___/___/_____

MY TRADITIONAL KARATE PATHWAY

# STRENGTH, SKILL AND KNOWLEDGE

# MY KARATE JOURNEY

## MY 100 DAY JOURNAL

My important dates, events, key points from lessons and memories.

_____

_____

_____

_____ Date___/___/____

_____

_____

_____

_____ Date___/___/____

_____

_____

_____

_____ Date___/___/____

_____

_____

_____

_____ Date___/___/____

MY TRADITIONAL KARATE PATHWAY
# STRENGTH, SKILL AND KNOWLEDGE

# MY KARATE JOURNEY

## MY 100 DAY JOURNAL

My important dates, events, key points from lessons and memories.

Date ___/___/_____

Date ___/___/_____

Date ___/___/_____

Date ___/___/_____

MY TRADITIONAL KARATE PATHWAY

# STRENGTH, SKILL AND KNOWLEDGE

# MY KARATE JOURNEY

## MY 100 DAY JOURNAL

My important dates, events, key points from lessons and memories.

Date ___/___/_____

Date ___/___/_____

Date ___/___/_____

Date ___/___/_____

MY TRADITIONAL KARATE PATHWAY

# STRENGTH, SKILL AND KNOWLEDGE

# MY KARATE JOURNEY

# MY 100 DAY JOURNAL

My important dates, events, key points from lessons and memories.

_____
_____
_____
_____
_____Date___/___/_____
_____
_____
_____
_____Date___/___/_____
_____
_____
_____
_____Date___/___/_____
_____
_____
_____
_____Date___/___/_____
_____

MY TRADITIONAL KARATE PATHWAY
# STRENGTH, SKILL AND KNOWLEDGE

# MY KARATE JOURNEY

## MY 100 DAY JOURNAL

My important dates, events, key points from lessons and memories.

_____
_____
_____
_____
_____
_____ Date ___/___/_____

_____
_____
_____
_____ Date ___/___/_____

_____
_____
_____
_____ Date ___/___/_____

_____
_____
_____
_____ Date ___/___/_____

MY TRADITIONAL KARATE PATHWAY

# STRENGTH, SKILL AND KNOWLEDGE

# MY KARATE JOURNEY

## MY 100 DAY JOURNAL

My important dates, events, key points from lessons and memories.

Date ___/___/_____

Date ___/___/_____

Date ___/___/_____

Date ___/___/_____

MY TRADITIONAL KARATE PATHWAY

# STRENGTH, SKILL AND KNOWLEDGE

# MY KARATE JOURNEY

## MY 100 DAY JOURNAL

My important dates, events, key points from lessons and memories.

Date ___/___/_____

Date ___/___/_____

Date ___/___/_____

Date ___/___/_____

MY TRADITIONAL KARATE PATHWAY
STRENGTH, SKILL AND KNOWLEDGE

# MY KARATE JOURNEY

## MY 100 DAY JOURNAL

My important dates, events, key points from lessons and memories.

Date___/___/_____

Date___/___/_____

Date___/___/_____

Date___/___/_____

MY TRADITIONAL KARATE PATHWAY
# STRENGTH, SKILL AND KNOWLEDGE

# MY KARATE JOURNEY

## MY 100 DAY JOURNAL

My important dates, events, key points from lessons and memories.

Date ___/___/_____

Date ___/___/_____

Date ___/___/_____

Date ___/___/_____

MY TRADITIONAL KARATE PATHWAY

# STRENGTH, SKILL AND KNOWLEDGE

# MY KARATE JOURNEY

## MY 100 DAY JOURNAL

My important dates, events, key points from lessons and memories.

Date ___/___/_____

Date ___/___/_____

Date ___/___/_____

Date ___/___/_____

MY TRADITIONAL KARATE PATHWAY

# STRENGTH, SKILL AND KNOWLEDGE

# MY KARATE JOURNEY

## MY 100 DAY JOURNAL

My important dates, events, key points from lessons and memories.

_____
_____
_____
_____ Date___/___/_____
_____
_____
_____ Date___/___/_____
_____
_____
_____ Date___/___/_____
_____
_____
_____ Date___/___/_____

MY TRADITIONAL KARATE PATHWAY

# STRENGTH, SKILL AND KNOWLEDGE

# MY KARATE JOURNEY

## MY 100 DAY JOURNAL

My important dates, events, key points from lessons and memories.

Date ___/___/_____

Date ___/___/_____

Date ___/___/_____

Date ___/___/_____

MY TRADITIONAL KARATE PATHWAY
# STRENGTH, SKILL AND KNOWLEDGE

# MY KARATE JOURNEY

## MY 100 DAY JOURNAL

My important dates, events, key points from lessons and memories.

Date___/___/___

Date___/___/___

Date___/___/___

Date___/___/___

MY TRADITIONAL KARATE PATHWAY
STRENGTH, SKILL AND KNOWLEDGE

# MY KARATE JOURNEY

## MY 100 DAY JOURNAL

My important dates, events, key points from lessons and memories.

Date ___/___/___

Date ___/___/___

Date ___/___/___

Date ___/___/___

MY TRADITIONAL KARATE PATHWAY

# STRENGTH, SKILL AND KNOWLEDGE

# MY KARATE JOURNEY

## MY 100 DAY JOURNAL

My important dates, events, key points from lessons and memories.

Date____/____/_____

Date____/____/_____

Date____/____/_____

Date____/____/_____

MY TRADITIONAL KARATE PATHWAY

**STRENGTH, SKILL AND KNOWLEDGE**

# MY KARATE JOURNEY

## MY 100 DAY JOURNAL

My important dates, events, key points from lessons and memories.

Date ___/___/_____

Date ___/___/_____

Date ___/___/_____

Date ___/___/_____

MY TRADITIONAL KARATE PATHWAY

# STRENGTH, SKILL AND KNOWLEDGE

# MY KARATE JOURNEY

## MY 100 DAY JOURNAL

My important dates, events, key points from lessons and memories.

Date____/____/_____

Date____/____/_____

Date____/____/_____

Date____/____/_____

MY TRADITIONAL KARATE PATHWAY
STRENGTH, SKILL AND KNOWLEDGE

# MY KARATE JOURNEY

## MY 100 DAY JOURNAL

My important dates, events, key points from lessons and memories.

Date ___/___/_____

Date ___/___/_____

Date ___/___/_____

Date ___/___/_____

MY TRADITIONAL KARATE PATHWAY

# STRENGTH, SKILL AND KNOWLEDGE

# MY KARATE JOURNEY

# MY 100 DAY JOURNAL

My important dates, events, key points from lessons and memories.

Date ___/___/___

Date ___/___/___

Date ___/___/___

Date ___/___/___

MY TRADITIONAL KARATE PATHWAY
# STRENGTH, SKILL AND KNOWLEDGE

# MY KARATE JOURNEY

## MY 100 DAY JOURNAL

My important dates, events, key points from lessons and memories.

Date ___/___/_____

Date ___/___/_____

Date ___/___/_____

Date ___/___/_____

MY TRADITIONAL KARATE PATHWAY

# STRENGTH, SKILL AND KNOWLEDGE

# MY KARATE JOURNEY

## MY 100 DAY JOURNAL

My important dates, events, key points from lessons and memories.

Date ___/___/___

Date ___/___/___

Date ___/___/___

Date ___/___/___

MY TRADITIONAL KARATE PATHWAY

# STRENGTH, SKILL AND KNOWLEDGE

# MY KARATE JOURNEY

## MY 100 DAY JOURNAL

My important dates, events, key points from lessons and memories.

_____

_____

_____

_____ Date ___/___/_____

_____

_____

_____

_____ Date ___/___/_____

_____

_____

_____ Date ___/___/_____

_____

_____

_____

_____ Date ___/___/_____

MY TRADITIONAL KARATE PATHWAY

# STRENGTH, SKILL AND KNOWLEDGE

# MY KARATE JOURNEY

## MY 100 DAY JOURNAL

My important dates, events, key points from lessons and memories.

Date ___/___/___

Date ___/___/___

Date ___/___/___

Date ___/___/___

MY TRADITIONAL KARATE PATHWAY
# STRENGTH, SKILL AND KNOWLEDGE

# MY KARATE JOURNEY

## MY 100 DAY JOURNAL

My important dates, events, key points from lessons and memories.

Date____/____/_____

Date____/____/_____

Date____/____/_____

Date____/____/_____

MY TRADITIONAL KARATE PATHWAY
# STRENGTH, SKILL AND KNOWLEDGE

www.ingramcontent.com/pod-product-compliance
Lightning Source LLC
Chambersburg PA
CBHW061134010526
44107CB00068B/2932